THE CHEATERS:

THE WALTER SCOTT MURDER

To Margaret –
Peace + good health

Scottie Priesmeyer

April 24, 1997

Walter Scott as lead singer with Bob Kuban and the In-Men, [c. 1965].

THE CHEATERS
THE WALTER SCOTT MURDER

Look out for the cheater
Make way for the fool-hearted clown
Watch out for the cheater
He's gonna build you up just to let you down.

Scottie Priesmeyer

TULA PUBLISHING: ST. LOUIS

First edition
First printing, 1997
Published by Tula Publishing, Inc.
P.O. Box 1544
St. Peters, MO 63376

Photos: Courtesy of Kay and Walter Notheis, Bob Kuban, Bob DeAngelis, Mel Friedman, Dr. Mary Case, Mike Turken, Jim Williams, and the St. Charles County Sheriff's Department. Other photos taken by the author, with permission from each subject.

DISCLAIMER: All the information in this book has been taken from court transcripts, police reports/ statements, official documents, newspaper accounts, written correspondence, and taped interviews. Some names have been changed to protect the privacy of certain people who were not suspects in the murder investigation. Areas of dialogue, which have been taken from the above sources, may have been altered, created, or embellished upon for better readability, yet the context remains accurate for each said incident.

Library of Congress Catalog Card Number: 96-61234

ISBN 0-9654668-3-3

Art direction: Susan Gutnik

Printed in the United States of America

In memory of Walter Simon Notheis, Jr.
and Sharon Elaine Williams

ACKNOWLEDGEMENTS

I want to acknowledge the extraordinary support and cooperation of numerous people who assisted me in creating this book.

Walter Scott's parents, Kay and Walter Notheis, Sr., opened their home and hearts to me. I spent many days interviewing them about their son, from his infancy to his death. They also revealed the arduous task they faced in trying to get Walter's murder case to trial.

Other people gave me valuable information about Walter's personal life. They are Doris Blair, Walter's first wife; Ronnie and Joanne Notheis, Walter's brother and sister-in-law; Bob Kuban, bandleader and friend; Bob DeAngelis, Walter's best friend, and his wife, Diana; Tom and Toni Molkenbur, friends; Mike Krenski, Greg Hoeltzel, and Larry Smith, former band members; Mel Friedman, former manager and music producer; and Bill Brown, neighbor.

Because I wanted a complete portrayal of the people and events from all perspectives, I visited Jim Williams at the Potosi Correctional Center. I found him affable and willing to talk about many areas of his life, his family, JoAnn and her children, friends, and some of the events leading to his incarceration.

Although JoAnn Calcaterra Williams would not consent to a face-to-face interview, she did articulately express her thoughts in several telephone conversations. Her close friend, Betty Loui, met with me and gave me significant information about JoAnn and Jim.

After acquainting myself with the case via newspaper accounts and stacks of transcripts, I contacted Lt. Wes Simcox. As chief of the detective bureau for the St. Charles County Sheriff's Department, he allowed me complete access to boxes of files, documents, hospital records, autopsy and police reports, and pictures regarding the investigation, as well as many hours of interviews. Several other law officials also gave me details on the case, particularly, former St. Charles County Sheriff Ray Runyon and Detectives Ed Copeland and Walter Blankenship.

Dr. Mary Case provided me with important facts, as did the attorneys who tried the case: Tom Dittmeier, Mike Turken, and Don Wolff.

Several people who assisted me in other areas are Jackie Starkey, Michael Sewell, Suzanne Sierra, Jim Campbell, Tim Kneist, Dan Duncan, Susan Gutnik, and Mike Taylor.

My peer readers, Mark Dickherber, Gene Bulfin, Chuck Schroeder, Mike Krenski, and Karla Yannotta, offered vital honest criticism on numerous drafts.

To all of the above, a heartfelt thank you for your time, kindness, encouragement, and cooperation.

PREFACE

Some true-crime writers focus the brunt of information in their books on the actual police investigation. Others have a penchant for writing about the lengthy legal maneuverings leading up to an intense trial. While both of these areas are essential in a true-crime book, other writers, myself included, prefer to concentrate on doing a psychological study of the main people involved in a murder case.

In the 1960's I had not been a follower of Walter Scott when he was a popular performer in St. Louis, and I also knew little about the murder case. After a friend, Chuck Schroeder, persuaded me to write a book on this case, I did a brief overview on the events and became hooked. Within a few weeks I knew I had to write the story, and resigned from my tenured teaching position.

Why did I launch myself into extensive research, into a year of writing about murder, an act I consider deplorable? The only logical answer I derived is that I like to get into the heads and hearts of people to find out what motivates them. And in the

Walter Scott case, I wanted to discover how cheating, greed, and lust led to murder.

Because nothing is confined to strict black and white terms, this book depicts both complimentary and unflattering portrayals of certain people. At first, this aspect disturbed me, since I came to know and like many of the people I've written about, even those I did not personally meet, including the deceased victims. Yet, in order to maintain integrity, an honest representation was essential. Several people in this book gave into their shadow side and made some unwise and self-destructive choices. It's my firm belief that when someone commits an injustice towards another person, retribution in some form usually follows, whether immediately or years later.

I've met many wonderful people in the course of writing this book. With bits and pieces of information, they helped me to reveal real-life people and personalities behind cold documents and reports. My heart goes out to everyone who cared for and loved the two victims: their friends, their families, and especially, their children.

Scottie Priesmeyer
September, 1996

APRIL 10, 1987. An all-day rain ended as darkness settled over the southeast rural section of St. Charles County. The Missouri River separated gentle rolling hills and unpretentious lifestyles from the bustling hubbub of metropolitan St. Louis. Peeper frogs trilled from ponds and creeks. Nearby, a lone deer foraged on the edge of a thick line of trees. During the day, white and pink dogwoods stood out against the naked oaks and hickory and birch. Only the past week stark branches were beginning to unfurl their green leaves. A light wind blew across an adjacent winter wheat field, creating shallow rolling waves.

Within the confines of a yard, a small rabbit nibbled new shoots of clover, taking small hops closer and closer to a large flower planter filled with ragged dead burdock and chickweed. As it neared the octagonal planter, it raised its head and sniffed the spring air. Its eyes grew wide, alert. Every muscle tensed.

In the distance a caravan of car lights filtered into the quiet, rural area, illuminating the barren fields and nearby woods. Soon the steady whir of high-powered engines hummed louder and louder, and the whoosh of tires splashing through rain puddles on the black-topped road invaded the serenity of the evening. A barrage of police cars, a crime scene van, and a truck hauling mobile lights, converged to a split-level house at 5647 Gutermuth Road, lining the driveway and both sides of the road. As car doors slammed, the rabbit, momentarily frozen by the lights, dashed to the safety of nearby bushes. The deer bolted into the woods, and the peeper frogs instantly stopped their serenading.

Over twenty police officers, detectives and crime scene personnel emerged from their vehicles and began walking toward the back yard. Two police officers in jeans and windbreakers directed the truck with the mobile lights as it slowly backed up, closing in on the flower planter. With shovels in their hands, several officers in heavy-soled rubber boots then stepped over the pickets surrounding the planter and started to dig. Soon, piles of dirt and clumps of mud lay in large dome-shaped mounds.

Lt. Wes Simcox, co-commander of the St. Louis major case squad criminal investigation team, and Detective Walter Blankenship were standing in the driveway when a Channel Five news van slowed down.

The driver leaned out of the window. "Hey, what's going on?"

Simcox, a handsome, dark-haired man who stood over six foot four, walked up and stated, "Probably the scoop of the year. But what are you doing out here in the boonies?"

"We got lost. We're trying to find a school near here to film a meeting."

"I think you'd have a better story within the next half an hour if you stick around," said Wes.

That's all the news crew needed to hear. Soon their cameras and lights were out of the van and they all headed to the back of the house.

After ten more minutes of vigorous digging, the men's shovels soon met with a solid thud. Brushing away a thin layer of dirt, they saw several inches of concrete encased by large sections of cedar. No way a single man could move this eight hundred pounds of covering. Several strong officers took off their jackets, grabbed hold of the cedar and began dragging it to one side. Everyone formed a circle around the men. No one spoke. The men strained and pulled the concrete slab. At first, only a slit of an opening appeared. Slowly, the hole grew larger.

Simcox peered down and quietly uttered, "Holy shit, take a look at this!"

A foot encased by a maroon-colored sock greeted the onlookers.

"It's him. We've hit the jackpot! Come on, guys, let's get this damn lid all the way off and wait for Mary."

Once the men completely removed the concrete covering, they all stared down at a body floating two feet from the top of the cistern, bound up like a ham, hog-tied fashion, and wearing a blue and white jogging suit. The front of the head was almost totally immersed in the water, with just a portion of the skeletonized face turned sideways. Onlookers noticed that the head hung gingerly onto the spinal cord by a thin thread of sinew, ready to disconnect itself from the rest of the body with just the slightest jar.

Fifteen minutes later a tall, short-haired blond strode confidently across the back yard. Dr. Mary Case. The Chief Medical Examiner for St. Louis and St. Charles counties arrived to supervise the removal of the body from the cistern. Two officers carried over an elongated, wire basket used to retrieve bodies from rivers or lakes.

"Be careful," warned Case, "postmortem teeth fall out easily and I don't want them dropping to the bottom of the cistern."

Heeding her advice, the men carefully lowered the basket into the water and maneuvered it under the torso. Suddenly, the head broke free from the body and rolled further into the dark water. Case, who was kneeling by the side of the cistern, quickly reached both hands into the cool water, grabbed the head, jumped up, and held it close to her chest, guarding it as if she had just found a rare artifact in an Egyptian tomb.

Walking under a large mobile light, she stared at it. Only bits of tissue clung to the cheeks and chin. Obviously, visual identification was impossible. After placing it into a cardboard box, she walked back to the edge of the cistern to continue directing the officers in lifting the body out of the water.

As several men lifted the corpse out of its temporary grave and laid it on a piece of canvas, everyone again closed in for a better look. The body was tied with yellow rope, now faded and frayed after several years in the water. The rope wrapped twice around each wrist, binding the hands together. Then it went down the front of the body, wrapped twice under the knees and extended to the ankles, which were bound five times.

The bloated body looked like brownish-grey and white bread dough or clay. One officer compared it to a sea sponge.

A deputy asked Case, "Mary, what is that stuff on his body?"

"It's hydrolyzed fat. His skin has been decomposed a long time." Bending over the body, she lightly touched one of the legs. "It takes years for a body to change to this material."

As two men reached down to place the corpse in a body bag, Case advised them, "Watch it. This stuff can easily fall apart."

After sealing up the body and head, Case and her assistant drove back to the St. Louis County Medical Examiner facility, where she would perform an autopsy on the corpse the next day.

Someone started the generator to pump out the ten feet of water in the cistern. Once only a couple of feet remained, an officer donned hip-high waders and threw a rope ladder over the side. At the bottom he found several large concrete blocks, apparently used to weigh the body down, three spent .410 shells, and a sealed plastic bag containing credit cards and a driver's license. Simcox hoped the bag would reveal the identification of the body just taken out of the cistern. It did.

Simcox called two of his detectives on his police phone. "Okay, guys, take him into custody. We've got the body."

1943–1958. On February 7, 1943, Walter Simon Notheis, Jr., was born at Booth Memorial Hospital in St. Louis, Missouri, to Kay Johnson Notheis and Walter Notheis, Sr. Six months later, Walter's father joined the Navy to serve in World War II and didn't return home to his family for three years.

While her husband was gone, Kay lived most of the time with her in-laws, but her life centered on her baby son. Almost from his infancy, she would refer to him as Wally, a name he would later only allow his parents to call him.

She said, "He was an excellent baby, a little angel." If she wasn't rocking him or singing to him, she'd place him in the playpen, where he'd play contentedly for hours. Because she had a propensity for cleanliness, Wally would not be allowed to play on the floor until he reached three years old. This early conditioning strongly influenced Walter to later develop a fastidious trait regarding his appearance and personal belongings.

From the time Wally could talk, he sang. Once a month Kay and her young son would ride the bus to Cairo, Illinois, to visit her mother, Alma Johnson. To pass the time and keep little Wally amused, Kay read nursery rhymes to him; in turn, her round-faced two year old would sing them back to her.

When her husband came home after spending three years in the Pacific, India, France, and the Panama Canal, the total love and attention she gave to little Wally now had to be divided. During the three year interim while Walter had been serving in the war, his young son had become spoiled.

"Why is he still eating his food out of a baby jar?" asked Kay's husband after a few days back.

"Because he can't swallow his meat. He's tried, but gags and spits it out. So, I thought that even if he's still eating baby food, at least he's getting his protein."

"Well," drawled Walter, an unusually reticent man, "this is going to stop right now. I can see you've allowed him to do pretty much what he wants."

"That's not true. He's a good little boy, and although he's been slightly pampered since you've been gone, he obeys me just fine."

Kay, a feisty, strongheaded woman, had to learn how to compromise again if she wanted her marriage to work. And Walter had to realize that he needed to reacquaint himself with his family, especially his three year old son.

Besides trying to get their son to eat regular food and learn to swallow his meat, Kay and Walter also wanted to find a way to keep little Wally in bed at night. He had a fear of the dark, and he'd get up to seek the warm comfort of his mother's arms. After trying various tactics, none which worked, his parents bought a feathered Indian head bonnet, since they knew he had a fear of bird feathers. That night they placed it over his bed. Walter's eyes filled with fright. Kay said he never again climbed out of his bed once she and her husband tucked him in.

As a small child Walter never had a temper and didn't know how to fight back. If a playmate hit him or pushed him down, he'd run home crying to his mother. His "short fuse" didn't start to activate until he got into high school.

"I'm not going to have a sissy for a son!" Walter firmly told his wife.

After two or three similar incidents, Walter sat his son down at the kitchen table for a talk. "Wally, look me in the eyes."

Little Walter, his eyes still red-rimmed, blinked as he looked up at his dad.

"You're not to start any fights. But if someone starts one with you, I'd better not see you hightailing it home. Whatever you have to do to win, do it. Do you understand?"

Wally nodded. From that day on, he learned to become a scrapper if someone came after him, showing no mercy to the instigator.

▪ ▪ ▪

Shortly after Walter returned home from the war, Kay became pregnant. Wally was four years old when his brother, Ronnie, was born. In the 1940's women used to stay in the hospital for two weeks to recuperate after having a baby. Once home, they were still expected to get a lot of rest. So, Kay sent Wally to stay with her mother in Cairo, Illinois.

During his month visit, Wally went to work with his Uncle Roy one day. Already his bright smile charmed people. Many of his uncle's co-workers gathered around the blond-haired child. Even at four years old, Wally loved people doting on him, telling him how cute he was and asking him to sing for them.

First, he started singing "How Much Is That Doggie in the Window," followed by "The Old Lamp Lighter." Soon one man put a coin into Wally's small hand, then another and another. His blue eyes sparkled and his pockets jingled with his first earnings as a singer.

Returning back home to St. Louis, Wally found himself with a baby brother who competed for his mother's attention. The two boys would always have opposite traits. Wally liked to dress meticulously: well pressed clothes, shiny shoes and neatly combed hair. As soon as Ronnie dressed for a special occasion, his shirttail would be hanging out of his pants, he'd scuff his shoes, then rumple his hair with his fingers. Wally always aimed for stardom and lived a fast-paced lifestyle. Ronnie was satisfied doing manual labor and being a family man.

Because Wally had been greatly influenced by his mother's neatness and orderliness, he kept his side of the bedroom clean and organized, including his toys. Wally loved staging a battle scene with a set of cowboy and Indian figures. Although Ronnie wanted to play with his big brother, Wally usually refused to have much to do with him. To retaliate, Ronnie would discover the hidden figures and smash them. A fight would then ensue.

During the next decade, Wally continued to sing, whether it was by himself, for friends, or at family gatherings. When the family took vacations, he had to sing to every song on the car radio.

"Mom, tell Wally to quit singing. I just want to listen to the radio without him always chiming in."

Kay would turn around, pat Ronnie on the knee, and reply, "Oh, let him sing. You never know. Someday your brother may become a famous singer."

Despite the disparities, despite the lack of closeness, if anyone tried to harm the other, they wouldn't hesitate to be there for each other.

■ ■ ■

Being staunch Catholics, young Walter attended St. Peter and Paul Elementary, and later, went to the all-boy Catholic high school, St. Mary's. In his freshmen year, he went out for football, track, and baseball. Although he broke his foot the first year of football, that didn't deter him from participating in the sport all four years. His long legs and quickness were also attributes for jumping the hurdles at track meets, where he earned many blue ribbons.

During high school Walter's popularity soared. He loved telling jokes, he loved being around people, and he loved having friends over to his house. Although Kay worked as a machine operator at Procter and Gamble and Walter operated a crane at American Car Foundry (ACF), they trusted their son implicitly and allowed him to have his friends over to the house after school.

A group of teenagers would come to the back door, take off their shoes, Kay's rule, then spend several hours dancing, playing cards, or just talking. Before they left, the trashcans had to be emptied, the glasses and snack bowl washed and put away, and the rugs taken out back to be shaken clean of crumbs. Then Walter, Jr., started supper.

▪ ▪ ▪

Because Walter always had an interest in singing and was already a member of a band, the Royaltones, he knew he wanted to make this his career. His father disapproved.

"Wally, you need to forget about trying to make a living singing. You'll never make it. You'll starve to death."

"No, I won't, Dad. I know I can make it big," responded the strong-headed teenager.

"Why don't you just be content getting an ordinary job? Anything but singing. You'll be up all night, living in the fast lane. What about having a family and settling down? Son, you just won't make it. The entertainment field is too tough."

"I don't want to do anything else. And I'll prove to you that I'll make it. Some day you'll see, and you and Mom will be so proud of me. I will be successful. And if I want to get married and have kids, I can make that work, too."

Walter, Sr., shook his head, knowing it would be difficult to convince his resolute son that he should forget about making show business his career choice. Ronnie said, "For the rest of Walter's life, this conversation lurked in my brother's memory. He had to prove to our parents that he could succeed as an entertainer and also have a family."

WINTER, 1959–SPRING, 1965. Around Christmas of 1959, Walter met his first wife, Doris, at a dance. Both were in high school. He was a sophomore; she, a junior. The first time she saw him, she thought he was the cutest boy she had ever seen. She liked his tallness, his sandy blond hair, his deeply cleft chin, and the letter sweater he was wearing.

He walked over to the table where Doris and her cousin, Barb, sat and introduced himself. Doris stood only five foot two, had long dark hair, and lively brown eyes. Her friendliness and quick laugh attracted Walter to her immediately.

A few days later she and Barb were sitting at a diner having a sandwich when Walter walked in.

Doris nudged Barb. "Isn't that Walter Notheis who just came in, the one we met at the dance?"

"Yeah, I'm going to call him over."

Doris's heart pounded as he came up to their table and sat down next to her.

"Hi, you're Doris, aren't you?"

She smiled and nodded, her eyes glinting with interest.

"What's your last name? I forgot?" asked Walter.

"Wucher."

"That's right. What are you doing here?"

"I'm studying before I go to work at St. Anthony's."

"Oh, yeah? What do you do there?"

"I'm a nurse's aid. I love my job, except sometimes it's tough finding time to catch up on my homework," Doris replied, pointing to several books next to her.

"So, I guess you come in here before going to work?"

"Yeah, usually."

This was the beginning of first love for both of them. Everyday after school they'd meet at the diner. After a few weeks, he asked if she would be his date at his sixteenth birthday party. She said yes. On February 7 her parents drove her over to the Notheis's house. It was their first official date.

A week later as she sat in the diner, Walter walked in, dropped his books down on the table and said he'd be right back.

Twenty minutes later he returned. She could tell he was both excited and nervous as he took a small box out of his coat pocket.

Opening it, he said, "I want to know if you'll wear this?"

Doris's eyes grew wide. It was an initial ring. She nodded and he slipped it onto her finger.

"It's kinda big and loose, but tape or wax should make it fit snugly."

She smiled shyly at him. "I guess this means we're going steady?" she asked.

Two years later Walter gave Doris an engagement ring. And on January 26, 1963, they were married at Holy Family Catholic Church.

Doris was pregnant.

The day they were married it snowed. But that didn't prevent a multitude of family members and friends from attending the wedding at eleven o'clock that morning. After they exchanged vows and shook the rice out of their hair and clothes, they drove over to Joe Tangaro's Restaurant for a late wedding breakfast. Following an afternoon of pictures and toasting champagne at her parents' house, they headed over to the American Legion Hall on Broadway for their reception.

It was after one o'clock in the morning when they finally pulled up to their small, newly furnished apartment. Because of the deep snow, Walter carried Doris to the door. Then once he opened it, he cradled his new bride in his arms again and crossed over the threshold.

For a couple of years they were happy, with only the usual minor arguments that most young married couples experience. In several months Walter would join the Bob Kuban band. Shortly after that, on September 1, 1963, Walter, III, would be born. Then Walter would meet JoAnn Calcaterra and his marriage would begin its demise.

▪ ▪ ▪

During high school Walter began taking his singing more seriously. He not only won first place in the annual amateur hour every year, but he also formed a band called the Royaltones. They would perform at some of the local taverns in south St. Louis city and at a few of his friends' parties. A short time later he joined another band called Bill Penneycook and the Pacemakers.

He was still singing with this band when Bob Kuban, a young local bandleader and drummer, came into a small club on Jefferson Street one night to hear Walter sing. Kuban's energy and passion for music overshadowed his five foot eight stature.

During the first break, he walked up to Walter and introduced himself. "Hey, man, you really have a great voice. In fact, I've been hearing you're the best male vocalist in St. Louis. If I'd close my eyes, I'd swear you're black. You have that rich, husky sound."

Walter laughed, brushing back his hair. "Thanks. So, you're Kuban. I've heard a lot about your band. Hear it has a great horn sound."

"Thanks. Yeah, we're starting to get quite a following. Listen, the reason I'm here is to see if you want to come out to Jackson Park and listen to us next Wednesday night. I'm replacing my lead singer, and if you like how my band sounds, I'd like to offer you the job."

▪ ▪ ▪

SUMMER, 1963. Pulling up in his turquoise and white 1955 Chevy at Jackson Park, Walter quickly slammed his car door and maneuvered his way through the crowd up to the band. Kuban spotted Walter and waved him over. At the end of the song he introduced him to everyone: Harry Simon, sax; Pat Hixon, trumpet; Skip Weisser, trombone; Ray Schulte, guitar; Mike Krenski, bass; and Greg Hoeltzel, keyboard.

Hoeltzel asked Walter, "What kind of things can you sing?"

"I like the R & B sound, like Wilson Pickett's 'In the Midnight Hour' and 'Soul Man' by Sam and Dave."

"What's your vocal range?" asked the guitarist.

Walter smiled. "I can sing just about any range."

The band members stared at Walter. Hixon then turned to Kuban and said, "Bob, if he's as good as you told us and can sing any range, why this could be our man."

Kuban grinned at Walter. "We've got a lot of gigs lined up. If you like what you hear tonight, we'd like you to join our band."

As the night progressed and the crowd grew to over one thousand, Walter was impressed by what he heard, especially the horns. Midway through the second set, Kuban invited him to sing a few tunes. And by the end of the evening, he agreed to become their lead singer. With Kuban's astute business sense and the talented musicians in the band, Walter's relative anonymity was about to end.

Although all of the members played with skill, being in a band was simply a way for most of them to earn money while getting through college. Hixon studied music at Washington University; Simon taught school and was also a graduate student at Washington University; Krenski attended Parks College, studying aeronautical engineering; both Weisser and Schulte were students at the St. Louis Institute of Music; and Hoeltzel attended dental school, also at Washington University. Even the bandleader and drummer, Bob Kuban would soon be graduating from college and had just signed a contract to teach music at Bishop DuBourg High School in St. Louis. Although he would be earning a steady income at his teaching job, the dream of having his own successful band always stayed foremost in his mind.

This was Walter's dream also. Walter wanted nothing else but to become successful through his voice. No college. No prestigious white-collar career. No desire to play an instrument. He just wanted to sing. Entertainment was more important to him than sleep, good food, or a sense of normalcy. And no one, nothing, would ever come between him and this goal.

As the band began playing for more teen towns, CYC (Catholic Youth Council) dances, and various clubs in and around St. Louis, its popularity steadily soared. The audience liked the "black" blues sound of the music and the deep, raspiness of Walter's voice. Because British bands were gaining a lot of attention in the United States, particularly the Beatles, the band changed its name from Bob Kuban and the Rhythm Masters to something more contemporary: Bob Kuban and the In-Men.

Also at this time, Walter developed a stage name. Because people had difficulty pronouncing Notheis, he decided to adopt "Scott" as his stage surname. Then to draw more attention to him, the band members decided to add one more touch to it.

"We need another 'hook,'" said Krenski, who was already writing songs for the band. "You need a name that will stand out from other lead singers."

"Yeah," chimed in Schulte, the lead guitarist. "We've tried 'Sir Walter Scott' but that sounds kind of hokey."

Walter puffed on his cigarette for several seconds, then his eyes lit up. "I've got it, guys! When I was in high school and started getting a lot of phone calls, at first my mom didn't know if the call was for my dad or me. So, she finally started asking if they wanted 'Big' Walter, my dad, or me, 'Little' Walter."

Kuban grinned. "That's it! Just like Little Richard. You can be Little Walter Scott."

▪ ▪ ▪

While the band practiced several times a week to tighten their music, they also included slapstick comedic routines, which the audience loved. Not only did Walter enjoy telling his corny jokes but most of the other members also appreciated old vaudeville humor.

Greg Hoeltzel and Mike Krenski wrote most of the schtick routines for the band, as well as much of its music. One act became a favorite for their audiences.

Hoeltzel would start by saying, "Isn't it a nice spring day? All those...flowers are blooming."

Krenski would respond, "What flowers?"

"I can't pronounce it right. Chrysanthemumiums...I mean, chrysanthenumumins."

"Oh," Krenski replied. "You mean chrysanthemums?"

"Yeah, that's it. You know, I can't say that stuff on the floor either."

Krenski would then look down on the stage floor and say, "Cigarette butts?"

"No! You know...linoliunumum."

"What?"

"I said...linoliunumum."

"Oh, linoleum!" Krenski would stare at Hoeltzel and say,

"Look, Greg, I can help you say it. Just pronounce one syllable at a time. Now repeat after me. La."

"La."

"No."

"No."

"Le," continued Krenski.

"Le."

"Um."

Hoeltzel would then pronounce the last syllable, "Um."

"There you go, Greg! Now say it altogether."

Hoeltzel would grin widely and loudly shout, "Chrysanthemums!"

Their young fans would hoot with laughter and then the band would get back into rock music.

▪ ▪ ▪

When first getting started, very few entertainers can solely rely on the income they receive from performing. Although Walter spent his nights going from one club to the next, he was recently married and had a small son to support. During the day he had a job at American Car Foundry as a crane operator. Two or three nights during the week and every weekend he sang in the band, not getting home until two, three, or four o'clock in the morning. The job at ACF started at seven. Consequently, he frequently reported late to his day job.

Greg Hoeltzel, the keyboardist in the band, said, "Walter insisted on maintaining a strong stage image. His clothes were always meticulous, his hair never out of place, and his aura was already that of a star." One day Walter had car trouble and called Hoeltzel for a ride from his job at ACF. As Hoeltzel waited for him in front of the factory, he was somewhat taken aback when he saw Walter walking out of the entrance gate with dirty pants and shirt, disheveled hair, carrying a lunchbox. He had never seen this more realistic side of the lead singer.

■ ■ ■

Being a newcomer to the band, Walter started out as a team player, arriving on time and helping to set up and tear down the equipment. As his popularity increased, so did his procrastination. Often, he entered a club just a few minutes before the band began playing. He knew it was his singing that had catapulted them to the growing success they were experiencing. The spotlight focused on him and he loved it.

Although he liked to joke around and had a good sense of humor, especially when he and the band members started to feel the crowd turn on to their music, he also loved to strut his lean six foot frame around the stage. The women loved it too. His blue eyes, deeply dimpled chin, and quick smile had many women pursuing him. His libido couldn't handle this strong temptation and he developed into a womanizer. Many nights his wife, Doris, recalled that Walter wouldn't get home until almost sunrise. Many times the phone would ring during the night.

"Hi. Is Walter there?" a young, female voice would ask.

Doris would turn over and shake Walter. "Another call for you," she'd say, handing him the receiver.

"Hello. Uh, huh. Uh, huh. No. Uh, huh. Bye."

"Who was that?" asked Doris.

"One of the waitresses asking if I knew where her boyfriend was."

"Why did she call you at three in the morning?"

"Who knows?" Leaning over, he'd give Doris a kiss on the cheek, then he'd roll over and go back to sleep.

Walter always had an alibi, a ready excuse, and because Doris loved and trusted her husband so much, she naively believed him.

▪ ▪ ▪

Despite Walter's and the band's popularity, Kuban made sure his members maintained a squeaky-clean image. Not only did they have to keep their hair relatively short and always wear clean, well-pressed button-down shirts, slacks, and cardigan sweaters, but he also would not tolerate any drugs whatsoever. From the first day he hired a new member, the one rule he stressed was that if anyone was found doing drugs of any kind, he or she would be fired immediately. Since Walter was never known to do drugs nor drink to excess, this was not a problem.

Although drugs were not a part of Walter's lifestyle, he tended to be extremely wary, overly cautious. Whenever he went into a room, whether it was a club where they were playing or a restaurant, Walter stood in the doorway and quickly scanned the situation. He also never put his back to anyone. When he would eat out at a restaurant, he'd always take a seat with his back to the wall. And from the time he joined the Kuban band, he never went anywhere without one of his handguns. When he wasn't playing on stage, he'd stick it under his shirt in back of his pants. On stage, he kept it either in a black bag or a briefcase and placed it nearby, within easy reach.

Some people who knew him said it was his semi-tough image of being brought up in the blue-collar section of south St. Louis that emitted this trait in him. Others said because of his propensity for philandering, he often had jealous boyfriends or husbands threatening him. Whatever the reason, until he died, he was suspicious about his surroundings and most people.

▪ ▪ ▪

In 1965 the band not only played at the St. Louis Playboy Club, the Gaslight Square area, wedding receptions and festivals around metropolitan St. Louis, but they also played at the Cardinal baseball games and at the annual Shriner's Circus. Their manager, Mel Friedman, who also owned the franchise of the St. Louis Playboy Club, kept them steadily booked. But they wanted more than local success. And they knew that the only way to achieve national stature would be to write a song that would rocket them to the top ten on the charts. In another year they would have their dream realized.

1939–1956. James Howard Williams was born on January 15, 1939. His mother, Gladys Corene Neal Williams, would not establish a close bond with her son until later in his life. Despite many promises to Jim's mother to quit drinking and to stop chasing women, Howard Thorne Williams, Jim's father, could not keep them. By the time Jim was a year old, his parents divorced. His mother took him to live with her in-laws, then she left the area. As a toddler, he began calling his paternal grandparents, Jessie and Clarence Williams "Mama" and "Papa."

His grandparents owned a two hundred acre farm and sharecropped two thousand more acres in Vincennes, Indiana, sixty miles north of Evansville. Besides raising milk cows, hogs, and sheep, his grandparents also grew corn, wheat, cantaloupe, watermelon, strawberries and tomatoes. From the time Jim was a small child, he had numerous farm chores to tend to daily. His grandparents expected Jim to gather eggs from the hen house and clean them first thing in the morning. Then he had to help herd the cows into the barn for milking. When that was done, he often accompanied his grandfather on his tractor or combine to tend the crops. The love he felt for his grandparents grew stronger each year.

Although he didn't have his biological parents to help him feel a sense of family, his aunts, uncles, and cousins frequently visited the Williams farm. Every other Sunday after attending Trinity Baptist Church, they'd assemble at the farm for a large mid-day meal. The table would be laden with several fried chickens, roast beef or ham, whipped potatoes, milk gravy, three or four types of fresh vegetables, homemade bread, fresh iced-cold milk, and two or three kinds of pies for dessert. Jim was well fed.

On Saturdays he and his grandpa would go to town to grocery shop. One of the things his grandfather would buy from the butcher was a couple of pounds of bologna. Later, on Sunday evenings when everyone had gone home, Jim didn't want any of the delicious leftovers. Instead, he and his grandpa would head into the kitchen and make themselves several sandwiches each, with three or four pieces of bologna, a layer of sliced tomatoes, topped by lettuce and smothered in mayonnaise. For years it was one of the weekly routines which he looked forward to with great anticipation. Another favorite meal of Jim's was hog brains, deep fried with lots of onions.

Being somewhat separated from other children, since he lived a mile from his closest playmate, his grandparents bought Jim a small horse when he turned five. Like most kids that age, playing cowboys developed into a favorite pastime. After the chores were done, he'd put on his cowboy hat, strap a holster with a cap pistol around his waist, jump on his horse and take off across the fields or down the solidly packed dirt road.

On their weekly excursions into town, while his grandfather visited with other farmers at the local diner, Jim would walk over to the local theater and watch the latest western. Later in the day after getting back to the farm, he would saddle his horse and pretend to be whatever cowboy he had seen on the screen that day: Gene Autry, Roy Rogers, or Hopalong Cassidy.

When he didn't ride his horse or play cowboys, Jim and his grandfather loved to fish at several small ponds on the farm or hunt rabbits. His grandfather not only became Jim's surrogate father, but also his best friend. Often, after the evening meal, his grandfather would head outdoors to smoke his cigar. Jim and his dog would follow. They would sit under one of the large trees near the house and watch the sunset. During these quiet moments at the close of the day, Jim's grandfather would often philosophize about life.

"You know, son, it's important to learn how to get along with a lot of different kinds of people. There's no one better than anyone else. Remember that."

"What about Mr. Hager down the road? He's so mean. Always yelling at everyone who steps foot on his property. How can anyone get along with him?"

His grandfather rolled the tip of his cigar around the inside of his mouth and looked at young Jim. "Always a reason why a man acts like he does. A long time ago Sam Hager lost his wife and three children in a fire. He's never been the same since."

Jim looked thoughtfully at his grandfather. "I didn't know that." After a few seconds of silence, he asked, "Why didn't he get married again?"

"With some men, once they find that special woman, there's no one else, no matter how good looking, no matter how nice, who could take her place."

Throughout Jim's youth, his Grandpa Williams would continue to tell him how to enjoy life, how to get along with people, and how to work hard to get what he wanted. In order to earn money to buy something special, his grandfather would give him a newborn lamb to raise. Once it matured and he took it to market, he could keep whatever money it brought. In this way, he could buy a new saddle for his horse, or when he got into his teens, a new suit for special occasions.

■ ■ ■

Although Jim would see his mother two or three times a year when she'd come to visit for a few days, his real mother was his Grandma Williams. She made sure he was well fed and learned good table manners. At night she tucked him into bed with a hug and a kiss. In her fifties, she died of cancer. Jim was eight years old.

His two aunts took over the maternal role. Fay, who was slightly retarded, had always lived in the household and knew how to run it. His other aunt, Mary Catherine, nicknamed Tootie, worked in a feed store in town and lived there during the week. On weekends she'd return to the farm. Although she was an attractive young woman, fifteen years older than Jim, she was also a tomboy.

After Saturday morning chores, he and Tootie would saddle up their horses and head out for a long ride. Giving her mare a good kick in the sides and hugging its mane, she would loudly laugh as her horse galloped across a field.

When Jim turned ten years old, his interests focused on sports, especially basketball. He was a tall boy for his age and he hoped to become a basketball star once he reached high school. After lunch or dinner, he'd practice. His grandfather nailed an old tomato basket to the side of the barn, and his Aunt Fay crocheted a net for it. For hours he would bounce his basketball on the bare ground by the barn door and swish it through the tomato basket. By the time he entered the eighth grade he was well over six feet. The next year, when he started high school, he played guard on the varsity basketball team.

His grandpa would attend his games and sit in the bleachers, cheering when his grandson made a basket, or yelling at the referees when they made a bad call against Jim's team. He was just as proud as all the fathers watching the boys dribble and pass the ball up and down the court as they tried to out-shoot and out-guard the opposing team.

"Hey, Clarence," drawled a friend during one of the games. "Your grandson is sure a fine player. If he keeps learning the game, he might get a scholarship to some college."

In fact, in his junior year Indiana University scouted Jim for possible recruitment the following year. But within the next few months, his biological father wanted a closer relationship with his oldest son and entreated him to come to Marion, Illinois, to live with him and his second family.

"Grandpa, I don't want to leave you. You were the one who raised me, not him. Now he just wants to push his way into my life and take over."

Grandpa Williams sat back on the porch swing, smoking his nightly cigar and staring across the cornfields.

"Son, comes a time in a boy's life when he faces a tough decision that can make him a man. You've been kinda sheltered here on the farm. It might do you good to try city life."

"But what about you? And what about my chances of getting that basketball scholarship?"

"I'm not going anywhere. Maybe you could stay there during the week and on the weekends come back here. I could use your help slaughtering the hogs, cutting firewood, and mending fencelines."

"But what about basketball?"

"Son, you're good, darn good. But do you think you're suited for college? You know farm work. You know how to use your hands. Do you think you want to be studying all the time? Think you want some white-collar job?"

Jim pondered. He liked to read, but he'd rather be building something, working with his hands. All his life his grandfather gave him excellent advice. Maybe city life wouldn't be too bad. More people. More things to do. And he'd be back at the farm on most weekends.

Although Jim would miss his grandfather, his aunts, and country life, he agreed to move to Marion, Illinois, and try to form a bond with his father.

1956–1963. In late summer of 1956, Jim moved in with his biological father, Howard Thorne Williams. Although his father had kept sporadic contact with Jim for seventeen years, he really didn't know his son. Howard had been remarried for many years and had other children by his second wife. When Jim came to the household, it was his first exposure to living with an actual parent and siblings.

His father, who resembled Jackie Gleason, had a good job with the coal mines as a purchasing agent. Although his father tried to make up for the lost years of seldom visiting his oldest son, it was a difficult transition for everyone.

After the newness wore off, his father proved to be a strict disciplinarian and still drank to excess. Jim already stood six foot six and weighed two twenty. Despite his gentle friendliness, no one wanted to mess with him. Once, when his father began to whip Jim's half-brother, Eddie, for failing a test, Jim stepped between them and grabbed his father's hand.

"Stop hitting him."

"Stay out of it," yelled his father. "This is between me and Eddie. If he brings home bad grades, he's going to get a beating."

"Hold on and listen to me," shouted Jim, towering over his father. "You know and I know that Grandpa Williams raised me and has been like my real father all my life. He taught me that like a horse you can't beat what you want into anyone, anything. He never even yelled at me in seventeen years, and I did what he wanted. Now lay off Eddie. It won't do no good."

His father's face turned crimson. "Mind your own damn business! And don't tell me what to do. Now get the fuck out of my way!"

Jim's eyes narrowed into tiny slits. In a hushed, menacing voice he told his father, "You'll have to fight me to get to Eddie, old man."

His father stared up at his oldest son. Several tense seconds passed as they glared at one another. Then his father gruffily said, "Ah, the hell with both of you." He grabbed a jacket and left the house.

After that, his father stopped beating his brother. Unfortunately, Jim learned some abusive traits from his biological father, and later on when he became a father, he whipped his two boys for lying about their grades, as well as for other infractions.

On week nights after school, Jim worked at the local Kroger store bagging groceries. When weekends came, he would head back to Vincennes, Indiana, to see his grandpa and help harvest crops and slaughter hogs. This continued until he started getting serious about a girl he had met at school.

▪ ▪ ▪

The first day of school he rode the bus. In the 1950's full skirts with crinoline petticoats were popular with teenage girls. As Jim walked down the bus aisle, he tripped over a girl's billowing skirt.

"Hey, why don't you look where you're going?" she snipped.

"And why don't you get your dress out of the aisle?" retorted Jim.

Sitting a seat behind her on the other side of the aisle, Jim looked her over. She had long, light brown hair with blond highlights, a dark tan, a pretty face, and she was tall, at least five foot ten. Besides this, she spoke her mind. Jim liked that in people.

When Jim got on the bus for the ride back home, the only seat not taken was beside this same girl.

"I see you got your dress out of the aisle," he said with a slight laugh. "Mind if I sit here?"

She smiled and scooted closer to the window.

"My name's Jim Williams. I just moved here. What's yours?"

"Sharon."

And so the initial awkward meeting settled into finding out more about each other.

Within a few months, Jim not only dated Sharon, but also several other girls from Marion. One day Sharon asked, "Well, Jim, is it going to be me or all those other girls?"

"What are you trying to say? That you want to go steady?"

"That's right."

Jim got quiet, then replied, "Let me think about this."

The next afternoon, he drove over to Sharon's house. As he pulled his 1954 candy-apple red Oldsmobile into the driveway, he saw her on the front porch doing homework.

"Hi. What are you doing here?"

"Well, I thought you might want to go steady."

In less than two years, on July 9, 1958, they were married.

▪ ▪ ▪

Soon after high school, Jim joined the Navy and was stationed in California, where he attended radio electronics school. When he came home on a thirty-day leave, they were married. Jim was nineteen; Sharon, seventeen. Within a few weeks, the Navy shipped him to Midway Island for thirteen months. Sharon stayed in Marion with her parents.

When he returned to the States, the Navy reassigned him to Coos Bay, Oregon. Sharon joined him and soon became pregnant. Because she was exceptionally close to her mother, and having her first child in a strange place overwhelmed her, she decided it would be better if she returned to Marion, Illinois, until after the birth of their baby. On March 5, 1960, James Howard Williams, Jr., better known as Jimi, was born.

Jim, a proud father and happy husband, drove his wife and newborn son back to Oregon to be with him. But after six months, Sharon again became so homesick for her parents that she and little Jimi headed back to Marion. Jim had one more year to serve in the Navy. Although they saved money for when he got out of the service, he missed his wife and son. The bonding he had felt with young Jimi began to sever, never to be fully mended.

▪ ▪ ▪

A year later the Navy honorably discharged Jim and he returned to Marion. He applied the money he had saved while living on base in Oregon to a new mobile home. For a year Jim worked various jobs, but nothing that brought in the income he wanted. Sharon's cousin had just moved to St. Louis to work for the McDonnell-Douglas Aircraft Corporation and was making good money. Jim also considered a move to St. Louis. One night he had a long talk with Sharon.

"Listen, babe, I can't find a good paying job here in Marion. I have a lot of electronic skills and can make decent money in St. Louis."

"Jim, I love it here. And you know how close Mom and I are. I don't want to leave her."

Jim's ire quickly erupted. "Damnit, Sharon. We're married now. We have our own family. I'm the one who has to bring the money in to support us, and I can't find what I need around here."

"But I don't like big cities."

Calming down, Jim put his arm around his wife. "Honey, we don't have to live in the city. We can find a nice, quiet place away from all the bustle. And we won't be that far from here, only a hundred and fifty miles. Why we could come back here every other weekend to see Mom and Dad. Besides, you could call your folks anytime you want."

Sharon lay her head against Jim's chest and sighed. After a few seconds, she tilted her head back and looked into Jim's brown eyes. "Promise me we can come back every other weekend?"

Hugging her closer to him, he whispered, "Yes, babe. I need you with me, but I also need to get out of here."

▪ ▪ ▪

Jim began working for the McDonnell-Douglas Corporation in St. Louis, where the company assigned him to the F-15 and Gemini projects. In February, 1963, he moved his family and their trailer to north St. Charles into a mobile home park close to the Missouri River. A year later on Jimi's fourth birthday, March 5, 1964, Sharon gave birth to their second son, Brett. Less than fifteen miles away, Walter Scott's voice helped create a large following for the Kuban band.

Summer–Fall, 1965. Because the Bob Kuban band had played at numerous dances for teenagers throughout the St. Louis area, by the time these young adults turned twenty-one, they had become loyal fans of the band. Since Walter Notheis, now known as Little Walter Scott, joined Kuban, the group became the top band in the St. Louis area. Walter's good looks, stage presence, and fine voice made him a strong front-man. His audience loved the music and they loved him. But the band wanted more.

Mike Krenski, the band's bass guitarist, still attended Parks College, but his real love centered on music. From the time he turned thirteen, he had written songs and he knew the difference between a successful local band and a nationally famous one was a hit record.

For several weeks he mulled over ideas about what made a record successful. Krenski kept a card file on certain songs and artists, and he began studying his notes. He knew there were many variables intertwined to create a strong hit song, yet all of them contained a hook. He concluded that many songs which made it big dealt with human traits, especially human frailties. After jotting down a myriad of weaknesses which people succumb to, he focused on cheating.

After several days of writing music and lyrics on a new song, he took it to the next practice. Hoeltzel, the keyboardist, readily conveyed to the other band members how it should be played. They practiced and practiced until it came together. Then Walter added his voice, and a unique sound developed. "The Cheater" was born.

The words to the song expressed how a guy, known as the cheater, would take away a girl from someone else, lie to her and mistreat her. This cheater was called a fool-hearted clown. He would make her feel like he'd give anything just to have her, but once he got her, he stopped caring. Later in the song, the lyrics told how some day the cheater would meet a girl who would know all about him and she would break his heart. Then everyone would laugh at him. The song ended with the cheater having tough luck.

▪ ▪ ▪

One night Kuban's band played backup with the nationally famous black musician, Curtis Mayfield. Several of the songs he made popular were "The Woman's Got Soul," "People Get Ready," and "It's All Right." Early in the morning, after the club doors closed, the Kuban band ran through Krenski's song for Mayfield. "It's not bad for white boys," he told them. He then proceeded to make a few suggestions on polishing it.

While trying to get Krenski's song refined enough for recording, the band continued their rigorous schedule. Half of the members still attended college during the day and played music at night. Several of the others worked full-time day jobs to supplement the band income. Because of their tight schedules, romantic relationships proved difficult to maintain for most of them.

Doris had returned to work several months after their young son was born. Soon afterwards, her parents gave them the down payment on a house, and they also replaced Walter's 1955 Chevy. Simultaneously, Walter's parents bought them a new washer and dryer.

Because he often overslept after performing until the early morning hours, Walter continued to be habitually late for his day job. Three or four hours of sleep a night didn't suffice. His eyes glazed with fatigue. His body craved rest. But he had to prove he could make it as an entertainer and so he pushed himself harder and harder.

On a rare night when he didn't perform, Doris would want to go out with her husband. Walter balked. Because he exuded high energy every time he was on stage, he wanted to stay home. The life of an entertainer rapidly tore at their marriage. After a couple of years, with Doris's encouragement, he finally quit ACF and directed his attention solely to his music.

The band occasionally performed at the popular nightspot where Ike and Tina Turner first started playing: the Club Imperial. One night as Walter was singing, he noticed one of the regular dancers, "little Tommy," with a tall, attractive brunette. Every woman who came into the club wanted to do the Imperial with this short, energetic middle-aged man. He knew all the smooth steps, even to twirling his partner over his back and between his legs. To contrast Tommy's dramatic style, his young partner depicted the epitome of cool. No smile, no expression whatsoever. She held her head high and her chest out. Her slender frame deftly followed each of Tommy's moves without faltering.

The next song Walter sang was one of Curtis Mayfield's popular songs, "Temptation's 'bout to Get Me." As he sang, he noticed the brunette with another partner, but now her eyes locked with Walter's. Still that impassive stare. He couldn't stop looking at her. There was something mysteriously intriguing behind her eyes.

At the break, Kuban came up to Walter and told him, "Hey, some hot young thing wants to meet you."

Walter, always willing to meet new women, said, "Sure, first let me get a club soda. I'll be right back."

When he returned to a table where the band members congregated with each other, their wives and girlfriends, there stood the tall brunette next to Bob. Walter smiled and walked up.

"Walter, this is JoAnn Calcaterra, a friend of mine," said Bob, introducing her.

JoAnn's stoic expression finally broke into a wide smile, revealing perfectly straight, white teeth. She was only nineteen years old.

▪ ▪ ▪

At seven o'clock the next morning, Kuban's mother came into his bedroom and gently shook his shoulders. "Bob, Doris is on the phone. Walter didn't come home last night and she's worried."

After telling Doris he'd check around, he pulled on a pair of jeans and a shirt, quickly backed his car out of the driveway and headed over to a place near Bellefontaine Road called The Cabins. It had a notorious reputation for accommodating clandestine affairs and quickies, a place, said Kuban, where Walter sometimes took women.

Seeing Walter's car, Kuban knocked on the motel door and heard muffled voices. Soon, the door opened. Walter's eyes bulged when he saw his bandleader. "Holy shit! What time is it?"

Peering around Walter's shoulder, Kuban saw JoAnn Calcaterra lying in bed with the sheets up to her chin.

"Doris called, man. She's worried. Better get on home."

Walter did go home to Doris, but from that day on JoAnn became a major part of his life until the night he was murdered.

▪ ▪ ▪

The manager of Bob Kuban and the In-Men, Mel Friedman, was also a record producer. When he heard Krenski's song,

"The Cheater," he had the band record it at Technisonic Studios on Brentwood Boulevard. Then he took it to some local St. Louis radio station directors and asked for feedback. They said the words in first person would make Walter look bad and suggested changing them to third person. Another suggestion was to quit trying to sound like a soul band, singing high falsetto harmonies, and go with their natural voices.

After the changes, Friedman put it on his local music label, Musicland, U.S.A. They then test marketed it with Bell Records. Soon, a larger subsidiary music publisher took over. All the stations played it. In St. Louis over twenty-five thousand records sold and the song soared to number one. By January, 1966, it reached number twelve on Billboard's charts, and for seven weeks it stayed in the top forty. The band was ecstatic. And Walter thought he finally would achieve the stardom he always craved.

January–August, 1966. After "The Cheater" became a national hit, the band put an album together. Soon, various clubs throughout the country booked them for special appearances. But their adrenaline really soared when the producer of the Dick Clark Show called Friedman and wanted them to perform on the highly acclaimed teen television show, "American Bandstand."

In the spring of 1966 they flew out to California. As soon as they stepped off the plane, their whirlwind tour began. They played at a popular club, Whiskey a-Go-Go, as well as on a soap opera, "Never Too Young." Performing at the Peppermint Lounge proved to be an eye-opener for these young midwestern men as a bevy of gorgeous topless waitresses served drinks to a packed house. Even the band's attorney, Art Poger, who was a bachelor at the time, joined the group on their tour and had a date with the beautiful, curvaceous Jill St. John.

Part of their tour also included Disneyland, where they sang at several promotional performances. As the band members walked across the amusement park, Poger stopped three teenage girls and asked them if they had heard of the song "The Cheater." They said sure. Poger then pointed to the musicians and told the girls, "These are the band members of Bob Kuban and the In-Men, and this is Walter Scott."

The girls stared at the good looking young men. One girl turned to Poger and sardonically replied, "Yeah, and I'm Mother Goose!"

The last night of their eight day trip, the band played at the Cow Palace in San Francisco. As their limousine pulled up in front of the building, they couldn't believe seeing "Bob Kuban and the In-Men" in large, bold letters on the marquee as the headline band. In small lettering two other groups were also listed: "Chicago" and then "Blood, Sweat, and Tears."

Although "The Cheater" sold only a half a million copies as of May, 1966, it still gained a lot of air-time on radio stations across the country, and eventually it even received some international recognition. But tension between some band members and Bob Kuban increased during the first half of the year. Kuban was not only the drummer but he was also the bandleader and a shrewd businessman. He paid his musicians slightly over scale, while he took most of the door money. This created dissension. Soon the guys began talking among themselves when Kuban wasn't around.

"We're doing just as much as Kuban, so why should we continue getting paid so little while he's pulling in the big bucks?" voiced Hoeltzel.

"Well, I don't want to seem too big-headed, but without me, Bob wouldn't be where we are today," chimed in Walter. "I think we could do just as well, if not better, if we split with this shit. Who's for getting our own band together?"

The members were divided. Schulte, the lead guitarist; Krenski, bass; Hoeltzel, keyboard; and Walter, the voice that made the band, all opted to leave. The other four members voted to stay. Kuban knew something was up since half the band members had begun to act aloof around him. Once they told him they were leaving his band, Kuban thought their manager and producer, Mel Friedman, instigated the breakup. But Friedman insisted that it was not his idea. Regardless of the reason, the band, which had the potential to make it big, dissolved in July of 1966.

▪ ▪ ▪

After hiring a drummer, Johnny Goodwin, who was also a law student, the new group came up with their name: the Guise. Soon, the band changed its name to "Walter Scott and the Guise," since Walter was the member who created a following. Krenski and Hoeltzel composed new songs and the band immediately began ideas for an album. Two of the songs, "Just You Wait" and "It's Been a Long, Long Time," had a great sound, similar to the style of the Righteous Brothers. Within a few months Bill Justice, a renowned sax player in the 1950's, expressed strong interest in the songs and was hired to arrange and record Walter and the band at Columbia Studios in Nashville.

Five band members and Friedman flew down in a small private plane. At the studio forty-five musicians and the Anita Kerr Singers were practicing for the band's scheduled recording session. After a twenty minute rehearsal, the lights dimmed and the red light came on. Everyone threw their sheet music on the floor and started in.

After both songs were released, Friedman arranged and produced the "Great Scott" album on the Musicland, U.S.A. label. Krenski and Hoeltzel wrote all but one song on this album.

▪ ▪ ▪

Bookings continued and numerous practice sessions were held at Walter and Doris's house. Doris didn't mind. She was friendly and enjoyed having the members over, and especially having her husband home where she knew where he was. For almost a year she was aware about his involvement with JoAnn. But Doris was now pregnant with their second child, and she thought the new baby would bring her and Walter closer together. It didn't.

▪ ▪ ▪

Numerous people who knew JoAnn stated that when JoAnn knew what she wanted, she went after it full force. And she wanted Walter for herself. While Walter was still working at ACF and she was a secretary for the KMOX television station in St. Louis, she would buy a carton of boiled, fresh shrimp and meet Walter out in the factory's parking lot for lunch. They would sit in his car eating, talking, kissing. If Walter stayed home with Doris and his son, JoAnn would slowly drive by, trying to catch a glimpse of him. When little Wally had his second birthday party, several family members and friends who attended said they saw her drive by a few times, park her car across the street and watch the house.

But occasionally tempers flared. Doris said after the band recorded "The Cheater," Walter and JoAnn had a serious argument, and he broke it off with her. About this time there was a big dance downtown St. Louis. He bought Doris a new dress and long gloves, and even reserved a room for the night at one of the finer hotels. As Doris and Walter sat at a table, one of their friends nudged Walter and pointed to the entrance of the room. There stood JoAnn. His anger igniting, Walter quickly scooted back his chair and headed over to her. Doris overheard him yelling at JoAnn.

"What in the hell are you doing here?" shouted Walter.

"I need to talk to you," replied JoAnn.

"No way. I want you to quit following me. I'm with my wife and I want you to leave me the hell alone."

"Can't we just talk for a few minutes outside. I needed to see you. I miss you, Walter."

"No!" Walter said firmly. "We're through. Can't you understand that? I don't want to see you again."

Despite his resolution not to continue his affair with JoAnn, he acquiesced to his strong attraction for her and resumed their fervent relationship a few weeks later.

▪ ▪ ▪

For several months Doris thought that things between her and Walter were going fine, except she noticed he wasn't wearing his wedding ring.

"Walter, where's your ring?"

"I've looked and looked, honey, but I can't find it."

Before, when she would ask him to wear his ring, he told her that he couldn't wear it while he sang because he had an image to maintain. But this time when he told her he misplaced it, she told him to get another one.

Soon after this incident, he asked her to take his suit to the cleaners. As she emptied out his suitcase, she found his wedding ring in the cuff of his pants. Although she got upset, she let it go.

In her seventh month of pregnancy, as Doris was again going to take a suit to the cleaners, she went through his pockets and found a postcard in his jacket. It was mailed from Florida and read: "Wish you were here. The sun is beautiful. I miss you and love you. JoAnn."

Several years later, Walter confessed to Doris that he purposely put JoAnn's postcard in his suit jacket because he didn't have the heart to tell her that JoAnn was back in his life.

Doris was furious. Yet having one small child and expecting the second in two months, she didn't know what to do; so, she allowed Walter to remain in the house.

▪ ▪ ▪

Walter also felt caught. He was in the powerful grip of an intense love affair, yet being raised a strong Catholic, he felt divorce was out of the question. He wanted to have both, his family and his lover.

September, 1966–October, 1969. Before Scotty was born, the tension between Doris and Walter chilled every corner of their house. Doris knew she couldn't be the type of condescending wife who was cognizant about her husband's affair but outwardly pretended it didn't exist. The emotional pain gnawed at her daily. Tears were commonplace. She loved Walter, yet to have him sleep in the same bed with her, knowing he was also making love to JoAnn, became too much of a burden.

One night several friends came over to play pool downstairs. The telephone rang. Doris was upstairs in the kitchen and answered it. When she said, "Hello," the other end clicked dead. Walter came up asking who called.

Doris stared at him, then sarcastically said, "Obviously someone who didn't want to speak to me."

Ten minutes later as Doris prepared a tray of snacks to take downstairs, the phone rang again. Walter bounded up the steps two at a time and got to the phone before his wife.

"Hi, yeah, uh-huh." After a slight pause, he said, "Can't

right now. Uh-huh. Talk to you later."

When he hung up, Doris stared him. "Who was that?"

"One of the guys from the club wanting me to play cards later tonight."

"You're lying. It was her, wasn't it?"

"Doris, damnit. Don't start in on me."

"It was her. I can tell by the look on your face."

Walter's eyes squinted in anger and his cheeks flushed with red splotches. "Can't you get off my back. Everytime I get on the phone, you start your bitching."

"I'm sick of your lies," yelled Doris. "I'm sick of her calling you here."

Suddenly, Walter raised his right arm, hauled back, and put his fist through the kitchen wall. Doris blanched and took a step backwards.

Still staring at her with heated eyes, he stalked past her. "I'm getting out of here. I don't need to take your shit."

Doris sat down on one of the kitchen chairs, covered her face with her hands and cried. She knew she couldn't take his cheating and lies much longer.

▪ ▪ ▪

When Scotty was born on September 14, 1966, Walter gave Doris two dozen red roses. As he held his second son, he glanced at Doris and smiled.

"We have another good looking boy, don't we?"

Doris nodded. "I think he's going to look like you, too."

"Can we name him Scott William and call him Scotty?"

"Sure. It's a good name."

For a few days all the tension dissolved between Doris and Walter. But it was short-lived.

Soon, Walter began staying out into the early morning hours, coming home smelling of a woman's perfume. Although he loved holding his newborn son and wrestling with his three year old on the living room floor, he was merely civil to Doris.

Doris would have long talks with Kay. Both were strong Catholics, but Kay firmly believed that once couples exchanged marital vows, they should stay married, regardless of rough situations. From the time Doris was sixteen, she had never loved any man but Walter. She still did. But she couldn't continue living with him, knowing that he was heavily involved with JoAnn.

Kay told her to wait it out, that Walter would come to his senses. Doris pondered over this. She thought no one else would want her now since she had two little kids. Although she wouldn't seek a divorce at this time, right after Scotty's christening, she asked Walter to move out.

"You know I love you, Walter, but I can't live like this anymore. Maybe if we have a trial separation for a couple of months, you can make up your mind who you want. Me or her."

"I don't want a divorce, Doris. I know I haven't treated you right the past year or so, but I do care about you. And you know how much I love our boys."

"I know you do. Let's just see how it goes."

"Where am I going to go? You know how tight the money is."

"I talked to your mom. She and Dad said you can stay with them for a while. This doesn't mean you can't see me or the boys. But I don't think it's a good idea to live together until you make up your mind. I just can't handle it anymore."

Walter packed up his clothes and moved in with his parents. But nothing alleviated his confusion. He continued to vacillate, wanting his wife, the mother of his two sons, but also wanting the enigmatic JoAnn.

▪ ▪ ▪

Within a year, not only did Walter's personal life alter greatly, but also during the summer of 1967, the Guise dispersed. Hoeltzel, the keyboardist, had just completed dental school and joined the Air Force to do his internship. The drummer,

Goodwin, finished law school, and he too wanted to begin his career. Several other members began evaluating their futures as musicians and decided that playing in a band had been fun when they were younger, yet being on the road created friction in relationships and most of them wanted to settle down. But singing was in Walter's blood. He had to continue.

Larry Smith, the bandleader for a group called the Kommotions, heard that the Guise had just split up. He had known Walter for several years. Although he knew Walter could not play an instrument nor read notes, he knew that Walter had a good ear for music to complement his great voice. Smith also had an energetic, beautiful female singer with his band, Holly Vaughn. She was only seventeen, but she already had a powerful voice. With both Holly and Walter as his lead singers, Smith knew the band would draw big crowds. When he approached Walter about joining the Kommotions, Walter took him up on it.

Despite the rumors he had heard about Walter's ego, Smith found his new lead singer easy to work with. Sure, he was strongheaded and assertive in how he thought certain songs should be played, but he also displayed a good sense of humor and loved to tell corny jokes. Like most of the band members, he only drank occasionally; and Smith reiterated what the other musicians stated: Walter did no drugs whatsoever. About the only thing Smith frequently discussed with Walter was his procrastination.

Walter was always late. The band would arrive an hour before performance to set up. Five minutes before they started playing, Walter would rush through the doors. Smith told Walter a few times that since they had an equal cut of pay, they should equally share setting up and tearing down equipment. The talks proved effective only on a short-term basis.

▪ ▪ ▪

In October, 1967, the band played at the Panorama Lounge in Belleville, Illinois, across the Mississippi River from St. Louis.

When Bob DeAngelis, a college student at McKendree College, saw Walter singing, he suddenly realized that Walter used to be the lead singer with the Kuban band. After the first show, he walked up and introduced himself. They immediately hit it off, and for the next sixteen years established a close friendship.

DeAngelis arranged for Walter and the Kommotions to sing at McKendree College in Lebanon, Illinois. This would be the first sit-down show that Walter would perform. Although it took a while to convince Walter to do it, he finally agreed.

When Walter arrived on campus, a taut, stiff expression supplanted his usual quick smile and friendliness. While he and the other band members set up the equipment, he put out one cigarette, only to light another within two minutes. His anxiety about the audience's reaction frayed his nerves. But once the horns, drums, guitars, and keyboard warmed up, so did Walter's confidence. He loved singing down and dirty blue-eyed soul, and soon he and Holly had everyone in the room clapping and shouting for more.

After DeAngelis graduated from college and began teaching history and language arts at a junior high school in Fairview Heights, Illinois, he asked Walter if he would come into his classes to speak about the entertainment field. Walter did. The students loved it, and Walter returned a few times over the next four years that DeAngelis taught school.

Eventually DeAngelis met his future wife, Diana. When they married, Walter was his best man. Shortly after this, DeAngelis left teaching and returned to his home state of New York. Despite the distance in miles, Walter and DeAngelis always maintained close contact by phone or visits.

▪ ▪ ▪

By the time Walter had joined the Kommotions he had been living with his parents for a year. He would see his two sons about once a month and would frequently talk to Doris.

In September of 1967, Kay and Walter decided to take a two week vacation. Although Wally had not spoken to his parents about moving out, Kay told her husband that by the time they got back, their older son would not be there.

Her premonition came true. He and JoAnn leased an apartment in the Cypress Gardens complex in north St. Louis County. For a while his life appeared more stable. He had a steady singing job and he lived with the woman he loved. She still worked for the television station, and she finally had the man she pursued for over two years in bed with her each night after his performances. The only hitch: he was still married.

▪ ▪ ▪

For the next year and a half, Walter sang with the Kommotions. Then he and Bob Kuban tried to pair up again. After several months of playing the clubs in Chicago, living in hotel rooms, and eating only restaurant food, Kuban had a talk with Walter.

"I hate the road. I want something steady in my life. Besides, I'm in love and want to get married. And, no way a marriage could work with my being gone so much. St. Louis may not be big time, but at least I think I'll be happier."

Walter tried it again on the road. After a few months of unsteady jobs, he too headed back to St. Louis. He rejoined the Kommotions, but money was tight. He worked part-time in the men's department of Stix, Baer, and Fuller, and he also drove a delivery truck for his manager, Mel Friedman, who owned several cleaners.

Around July of 1968 he was arranging some men's ties on a display table when suddenly a woman came up to him and gave him a big hug. It was his friend and former hairdresser, Toni DiGennaro.

"Toni, my God, I haven't seen you in over a year. What a great surprise!"

"Hi, you big lug! What are you doing working here? I

thought since 'The Cheater' made you a star that you'd be off to Hollywood and just forget about me."

"Things didn't work with Kuban and me. I formed another band but then most of the members graduated from college and left music. Right now I'm playing with the Kommotions. This job here is just part-time until I catch up on my bills. I guess you heard Doris and I separated a couple of years ago."

"Yeah. What happened? Weren't you and JoAnn getting to be a heavy item?"

"We're now living together over in Florissant." Looking at his watch, he said, "I'm taking a lunch break in half an hour. How about meeting me in the Tea Room and we can catch up on what's been going on?"

As they ate their lunches, Walter told Toni how much he loved JoAnn, that he had never met another woman like her. Then he leaned over and looked closely at his friend. "Hey, I see a new gleam in those bright Italian eyes of yours. You're in love, aren't you?"

Toni laughed. "You can still read me without my saying anything. Yes, I'm in love and engaged. See." She held out her left hand where a diamond shone on her ring finger.

"Who's the lucky guy?"

"His name is Tom Molkenbur. He's handsome, funny and sweet."

"I'm happy for you. Listen, you know how JoAnn is, somehow always finding out what I do, who I'm with, so I'd better call her this afternoon and tell her that I ran into you. How about the four of us getting together soon? I want to meet Tom."

In a few weeks the four of them got together one night and played miniature golf. Walter approved of Toni's fiance, Tom; and JoAnn and Toni began to develop a close friendship, which lasted many years. Soon, the four of them became inseparable friends and shared confidences.

FEBRUARY, 1969. Doris filed for divorce twice. But each time Walter would think of a final dissolution between him and his wife, he would panic and start calling and seeing her more. This created havoc and heartache for everyone. His mother would have frequent conversations with Doris's divorce attorney, Art Poger, telling him to delay the divorce as long as possible. She hoped her son would tire of his affair and return home to his wife and sons.

JoAnn became weary and irate. She might have Walter in her bed each night, but there was still the umbilical cord attached to his mother and his guilt as a Catholic attached to divorcing Doris. One day in February of 1969, she gave Walter an ultimatum, her or Doris. A fight ensued, and she packed up and left the apartment.

Later that evening, Walter called Doris and wanted her to come over to his apartment for a talk.

"You sound really down, Walter, but I can't just leave the boys to come over."

"Please. I want to talk to you about us."

"Not tonight. Why don't you sleep on this, and if you feel the same tomorrow night, come over here for supper."

The next night Walter went over to Doris's. After wrestling with his two sons on the living room floor, Doris and Walter tucked their children into bed, then they sat on the couch.

"I miss you and the boys, Doris. I want to try to work things out between us."

"What about JoAnn?"

"We're through. She packed up and left. I never want to see her again."

Doris sat quietly. She still loved Walter, despite his affair. Also, watching him play with their two boys melted down all her rationality.

"Okay, I'll give you one more chance."

He grabbed her, kissing her and holding her tightly. "Thank you, honey. You'll see, everything will work out fine and we can be a family again."

Walter convinced Doris to move into his apartment. The next day Kay and Walter came by Doris's to help pack the cars with clothes, bedding, some kitchen utensils and several lamps. Everyone smiled and joked around. The long wait for Walter to tire of JoAnn and want his family back had finally ended.

Doris rearranged the apartment, putting her things into unfamiliar cabinets, closets, and drawers. The two rambunctious boys clambered all over their father that first night together. When Doris fell asleep in Walter's arms, she felt as if the nightmare she had been through for over three years had been blotted out of her head.

It was merely a respite.

Two days later, early in the morning, Doris was crying when she called Kay. "That's it. Come up here and help me pack up. Walter didn't come home last night."

When she got back to the house, she called her lawyer. "Okay,

Art, go through with it. No backing out of it this time."

▪ ▪ ▪

April, 1969. Although Walter and JoAnn made up, he still felt bad about what he had done to sever his relationship with Doris. His parents raised him in a devout Catholic family where divorce was out of the question. His guilt ran rampant. Several times he tried to talk Doris out of the divorce, but she was adamant about ending their marriage.

This created further conflicts between Walter and JoAnn. She knew his dilemma, but she also felt that she couldn't continue in the relationship since he also blamed her for the situation. Therefore, when she ran into a former lover of hers, she began seeing him, and once more left Walter.

Toni was at work when her husband telephoned. "Honey, call Walter right away. He's crying and sounds real bad."

When Walter heard his friend's concern, his voice cracked and he was soon sobbing. "I can't live without her. My whole life is so fucked up that I'd be better off dead."

"Don't talk that way, Walter. You know she'll come back."

"Not this time. She's seeing an old boyfriend. I can't handle the thought of her in bed with anyone else."

As his despair deepened, he told her he planned taking a handful of pills. Toni immediately left her job and headed over to Walter's apartment. All night they talked and talked. Only when she thought she finally convinced him that things would be all right and he fell into a deep sleep, did she go home. Before leaving, she called Walter's parents, telling them about their son's condition. They told her they'd be over shortly.

A few minutes after Toni left, Walter woke up. His mind began churning again and the guilt he felt wound around his heart, tightening its grip. It was Easter Sunday, a time to be with family, a day he should be with his wife and sons. He felt he had no one.

When Kay called to tell him she and his dad were on their way, he told her he might shoot himself.

"Damnit, Wally, don't you dare! You stay away from that gun. Do you hear me? Your father and I are on our way over."

As they entered his apartment, Walter lay on the couch in a fetal position. His whole body shook uncontrollably, while guttural anguish echoed off the living room walls. Kay called her physician, Dr. McDonald, and he told them to get Walter over to the emergency room at St. Mary's Hospital. They admitted Walter for a nervous breakdown.

■ ■ ■

For over three weeks Walter remained in St. Mary's. He alternated from crying jags to catatonic behavior. Bob Kuban visited him several times, as did JoAnn. Everyday after teaching school, Bob DeAngelis drove from Fairview Heights, Illinois, to St. Louis. Kay and Walter also visited their son daily. Two or three times Doris came with her in-laws to see Walter, but the visits created such a negative reaction in him that the doctor finally suggested she not return.

The psychiatrist at the hospital said Walter suffered from an acute guilt trip. He wanted Doris because she was the mother of his sons, but he also wanted JoAnn because he loved her. The doctor added that Walter was the type of person who couldn't handle conflicts in a relationship very well. He said Walter would have to focus only on himself and his career as the number one priority in his life. Thereafter, he did.

On one of Kay's visits, Walter sat across from her. His eyes looked pleadingly at her. "Mother, I wish you'd tell me it's okay to get a divorce and marry JoAnn."

Kay shook her head. "I can't do that, Wally. That's your decision."

"But I love JoAnn so much."

Kay looked steadily at her older son. "Wally, if I loved your daddy as much as you say you love JoAnn, why I wouldn't care what anybody would say. I'd marry him. I'm the one that would have to live with him. Nobody else."

"But if I get divorced from Doris and marry JoAnn, I'll have to give you up."

"That's ridiculous! We love Doris and always will. We don't have to give her up just because you two will be divorced. Well, you wouldn't have to give us up either if you marry JoAnn. We'll still love you, but," she paused before continuing, "...but we don't have to give you our blessings."

Several days later, the doctor released Walter from St. Mary's. At noon, JoAnn picked him up.

▪ ▪ ▪

Because Walter's self-esteem had plummeted during his breakdown, he refused to sing. It took several more weeks before he slowly started having friends visit him more often.

Since early winter, DeAngelis's fraternity had been planning a large party at Fischer's Restaurant in Belleville, Illinois. Along with food and drinks, there would also be a band. He called Walter's parents to invite them over, and encouraged Walter and Doris to join them. Although Doris continued with her divorce petition, in order to cushion Walter's fragile emotions and lessen his guilt trip, she told him that if they felt differently about each other later on, they could always remarry.

When Walter arrived at the restaurant with his parents and Doris, he felt awkward. Then DeAngelis sat down next to him and Walter's tension decreased. After the band played a few songs, the bandleader took the microphone and headed over to Walter's table.

"Hey, ladies and gentlemen, look who's here with us tonight. The talented and popular singer of 'The Cheater,' Walter Scott."

Everyone stopped talking and turned to stare at Walter.

"Wouldn't all of you like to hear a few tunes from him?"

The audience clapped. At first Walter was reluctant, but DeAngelis said, "Walter, it's okay. Listen to them. They want to hear you sing, man."

Finally, Walter scooted back his chair, got up, and walked to the stage. Taking the microphone from the bandleader, he told the members several songs to play and they started in. Although he sang only four songs, it was enough to instill some of his confidence back.

Over the summer, Walter started putting another band together called Walter Scott and the Cheaters. In October of 1969, four years after he had met JoAnn Calcaterra, Walter and Doris were officially divorced.

October, 1969–August, 1972. After Walter formed his new band, Walter Scott and the Cheaters, his bookings escalated, and for weeks at a time he performed on the road. His increased confidence and the way he worked the audience assured him that he would succeed as an entertainer.

When he would be in St. Louis for a few days, he would visit his boys and Doris would invite him in. No longer did animosity envelop them. They could now laugh together as their two sons cut-up and hung onto their father. They could even get the scrapbook of old photos out and reminisce about old times.

On previous Christmas Eve's while they were separated, Walter would spend the night at Doris's, sleeping on the couch so he could see his sons get up early on Christmas morning and open their gifts. But on December 24, 1969, Walter would not be with his sons. That day, he and JoAnn exchanged marriage vows before a justice of peace at city hall. Three days later, he left for the road again.

■ ■ ■

For two years Walter's band played from Chicago to Wisconsin and up towards the east coast. Many rock groups in the early 1970's began to play heavy metal, wore long hair, and experimented with a variety of drugs, from pot to LSD. But Walter refused to succumb to this craze in order to achieve national stardom. His nightclub act exhibited class, not frenzied antics. Despite societal upheavals in the women's, civil rights, and anti-war movements, many Americans retained a stable sense of conservatism. These were the people who found Walter's act appealing, and he continued to draw large audiences wherever he performed.

■ ■ ■

Early in 1972, Walter called his first wife. "Guess what?"

Doris couldn't imagine why Walter was so ecstatic. "No telling with you, Walter. What is it?"

"JoAnn's pregnant. We're going to have twins!"

Doris was surprised. He told her several times after they had Scotty that he didn't want anymore children. He barely saw his first two sons. She wondered how he would handle two more.

On August 11, 1972, Mindy and Bryan Notheis were born.

1973–1975. Growing up on a farm and learning the values of hard work and responsibility at a young age, Jim Williams continued these ingrained principles as an adult. Although he continued to work the night shift at McDonnell's for eleven years, during the day he earned extra money doing odd jobs on the side: wiring houses and carpentry. Eventually, he thought he could make more money with the side work and quit his job in 1973.

For a brief period he supplemented his income by working for Broph's Mobile Home Sales. Because of his affable personality, he began making acquaintances with county and city officials. Soon, he was offered the position of electrical inspector for St. Charles County, which he readily accepted. His wife, Sharon, worked as a reservationist for Trans World Airlines. Between the two of them, they brought in a decent income for a family of four.

Both were outdoor people. Many weekends, they packed up the camper and headed to remote areas in Missouri, Illinois, and Arkansas. Jim and his sons, Jimi and Brett, would sit on the bank of a lake fishing, while Sharon would be nearby reading a book. When they weren't fishing, Jim and his boys would hunt rabbits.

As he had promised his wife, every other weekend they returned to Marion to visit Sharon's parents. Occasionally, he suggested taking a trip to Indiana to visit his father and stepmother, but she never wanted to go with him. She couldn't understand why he wanted to have anything to do with a father who had seldom been a part of his life until Jim turned seventeen years old. Jim's mother had since moved to Florida, so it was rare to visit with her. He said he didn't think much about his biological parents until he saw the closeness between Sharon and her mother. Then he began to realize what he had missed as a child. As he got older, he wanted to establish a better relationship with his parents, despite their apathy toward him when he was a youngster.

If Jim and his family didn't camp out or go to Marion, Illinois, on weekends, they enjoyed other interests. Sharon loved working on ceramics, which she would later sell at craft shows. Another favorite pastime of hers was sewing. Jim built her a sewing room, complete with various shelves for materials and small drawers for her threads, pins, buttons, and patterns.

People had often told Jim that he was a workaholic. He couldn't idly sit watching television for several hours. If he did watch a TV show with his family, he'd keep occupied by knitting or crocheting. But being an outside person, he preferred doing yard work and gardening. Each spring he would put in a large vegetable garden. Half of whatever it produced, he gave to friends and neighbors. In addition, Jim also loved to cook and bake. At Christmas or on birthdays, he would give his friends homemade lemon meringue pies or chocolate chip cookies.

Jim and Sharon were also involved with two active boys. Both were exceptionally large. Both loved baseball. Jim said his son, Jimi, possessed natural athletic skills and was one of the best young baseball players he had ever seen. Being only eleven, Jimi's coaches were amazed at his speed and accuracy when he pitched. But this was short-lived.

One night Jim had taken off work to watch his son play. As his older son stood on the mound, Jim noticed him limping; and when Jimi stretched his legs out to pitch, his son's face tightened up and his eyes winced in pain. After the game, Jim asked if he had gotten injured. Jimi said no, but added that his knees hurt him a lot. The next day Jim arranged for his son to see a orthopedic specialist. Diagnosis: Osgood-Schlatter's disease. Treatment: anti-inflammatory medication and no sports. This news devastated Jimi.

Instead of baseball, Jimi's interest soon turned to playing the drums. After school, he would go over to a friend's house and learn the fundamentals. That Christmas Eve, Jim spent hours putting together a new drum set for his son. In the morning, he and Sharon stood at the bottom of the stairs with a camera to take their son's picture when he would spot his gift. Jim said when Jimi saw his drums, he had the brightest smile and the happiest eyes he had ever seen on a child's face. It would be the last time he would ever see his older son with that look.

As with all families, they also had problems and arguments. Jim liked to dance; Sharon didn't. Yet whenever he would ask some other woman to dance, Sharon started to badger him with her jealousy. And usually she wouldn't wait until they were alone to voice her complaints. She said what was on her mind at the time. The trait he had originally admired in his wife now caused friction in their marriage. Jim also managed a women's softball team one year and Sharon accused him of sleeping with all of the players. Jim said she would look him in the eye and say, "If you're looking at it, you're sampling it."

▪ ▪ ▪

Although the arguments were over usual petty jealousies and differences of opinions, they soon amplified to serious proportions over Jimi. One afternoon Jim was in the front yard raking leaves when their new cocker spaniel pup came wriggling up to him with something in its mouth.

"Whatcha got, fella?" Jim took a plastic baggie out of the dog's mouth and his jaw dropped open. Pot. Soon, the pup came back with another bag. More pot. Following the dog to the back yard, he saw it crawl under a workshop area. Jim got down on all fours and saw a grocery bag. Hauling it out, he dumped the contents on the ground: four bricks of marijuana and numerous small bags of pot.

As a member of the Jaycees, he had gotten to know many St. Charles businessmen, judges, lawyers, doctors, and law enforcement people. Through this organization and others, he had also become friends with the Chief of Police of St. Charles. Jim went immediately into the house and placed a call to him.

"Gotta problem with my kid. Just found a bunch of marijuana he hid in the back."

"Want me to come out and get rid of it for you?"

"Hey, I've got a commode and can do the same thing here. No, I want something that will make Jimi think long and hard before he thinks of doing this shit again. What about that Scared Stiff program? Does it work?"

"Depends. Sometimes it does; sometimes it doesn't. How old is Jimi?"

"Fourteen. Thinks he's twenty-two." Jim hesitated for a moment, then took a deep breath and said, "How about coming out to arrest him, put him in jail for a short time to scare the shit out of him?"

"I can't arrest him because he's a juvenile. We could only hold him for questioning for a twenty hour period. Then you have to come get him."

"Yeah, let's do that. Keep him in overnight and I'll pick him up in the morning. It might teach him a lesson."

Jim called Sharon at work and told her about the incident and his plans to put Jimi in jail overnight. She agreed, thinking it could straighten him out before he got too involved with drugs.

When Jimi came home a short time later, Jim confronted his son. "Look what I stumbled across today," he said, pointing to the bag of pot.

Jimi's face blanched bone-white.

"Know anything about it?"

Jimi looked at his dad and nodded. "Yeah, it's mine."

About that time the police chief drove up.

"What's he doing here?" asked Jimi.

"He's taking you in for questioning. I'm going to teach you a lesson so you know never to deal drugs again."

The next morning Jim arrived at the city jail. A few minutes later his son came through the steel security door.

"How're doing, Jimi?"

Jimi, already over six feet, glared at his father and stuck his finger in Jim's face. "I'm going to tell you something right now, old man. One of these days I hope your ass will be behind bars. I'll never be the same after last night."

From that day on, instead of thwarting Jimi's propensity regarding drugs, his experience in jail intensified his illegal activities. And most of the arguments Jim and Sharon would have centered on Jimi. Jim was angry about where his son was heading; Sharon insisted that Jimi was basically a good kid but ran with a bad group of friends, and someday he'd straighten out.

▪ ▪ ▪

Establishing an acceptable method of training children to become responsible adults is an area of child rearing which many parents find frustrating. Kay and Walter, Sr., raised their two sons with a lot of love combined with discipline. When their son, Walter, was still married to Doris, he taught his boys the standards his parents instilled in him. They could not be rude and had to obey adults. But once he and Doris divorced, he wasn't around them often and Doris found it a struggle to continually discipline them. The rules relaxed and they became more rambunctious and spoiled.

The boys seldom saw their father, but when he did pick them up for a day or two, or for only a few hours, they knew they had to behave. One day Walter came back to St. Louis for a few days and visited his older son's classroom at St. John the Baptist. As Walter stood at his son's door, he saw Wally standing with his head in the corner. When the nun greeted Walter, his son turned around and loudly said, "Uh, oh, now I'm really in trouble!"

If Walter had his boys with him, sometimes he'd take them to a club and they would watch him rehearse. Other times he would take them to his house and they'd spend the night. At first, JoAnn treated them nicely and they enjoyed the visits. But after the twins were born, they thought she became overprotective regarding their half-siblings. Doris stated that the boys told her JoAnn wasn't mean to them, yet if they wanted to play with Mindy and Bryan and she thought they were too rough, she would make the boys stop playing with them altogether. On some visits, when the boys walked in the front door, JoAnn would quickly say hello, then leave with the twins for the rest of the day.

■ ■ ■

Although Doris had been emotionally distraught for years because of Walter's affair with JoAnn, a time came when her magnanimity was tested. Her younger son was making his first communion in the Catholic church. Grandparents, cousins, aunts, and uncles attended this important rite. Walter sat next to Doris; his new family sat a few pews back.

After the ceremony, Scotty came up to Doris and whispered, "Mom, can Dad come over to the house for cake and ice cream?"

"Sure, honey."

"Can, uh, JoAnn and the twins come too?"

Doris shrugged her shoulders. "Well, they came with your dad, didn't they?"

Back at the house, Doris was cutting the cake when Mindy and Bryan tugged at her dress and began talking to her. They were cute little three year olds and she had no animosity toward them, but it was an awkward situation. Here was the woman who took away her husband, standing across the room talking to Scotty. Something didn't seem right with the scene. That night she felt an emptiness in her heart.

■ ■ ■

Because Walter traveled so much, he didn't have much time to spend with his children. He would be gone for two or three months, then suddenly be back in St. Louis for a week or two, usually to change seasonal wardrobes. It was not a normal father-son relationship he had with his first two boys by Doris. Occasionally, if he performed at the St. Louis Playboy Club, Walter's parents would take their grandsons down to watch their father. But as time went by, the boys became occupied with their own interests and activities.

When Wally, Jr., was around twelve and Scotty nine, they had long planned to spend Bevo Day, an annual St. Louis event, with a group of their friends. The day before their father called. It had been five or six weeks since they had heard from him.

"Hey, guys, I'm in town. I'll pick you up in a little bit. You can spend the night and we'll do something all day tomorrow."

Wally, Jr., hesitantly said, "Dad, we have plans. We can't. How about a couple of days from now?"

"Change your plans. I can't do it except for today and tomorrow."

"Dad, we really want to go to Bevo Day with our friends tomorrow. Can't you change your plans?"

"So, these plans are more important than me, huh?"

"Dad, that's not it. But we've waited a long time for tomorrow."

"I don't care what you have planned, damnit. I'm coming over anyway. So, pack a bag. You and Scotty are staying with me."

For six hours Walter sat in his van outside of Doris's house. The boys would not come out. Doris had called her attorney and he told her that as long as the boys remained in the house, Walter couldn't force them to go with him.

Finally, she went out to talk with her ex-husband.

"Walter, the boys have had these plans for weeks. You can't just come in town without notice and suddenly expect them to drop whatever they're doing and go with you. They aren't little boys anymore."

"Well, something's not right. I see them when I can, and I always make sure they get a card and gifts on their birthdays and at Christmas. Yet I don't even get one rotten card. Absolutely nothing."

"Well, neither do I," exploded Doris. "And I'm the one who puts up with their arguments, fixes their meals, washes their clothes, takes care of them when they're sick, drives them to school functions and over to their friends. And, do I get a card or a gift? No!"

Walter became quiet. Taking a deep breath, he gazed at his ex-wife and said, "It's like I don't know my own sons anymore."

"You're not around them much, Walter. You have your career on the road, and they're growing up."

Walter looked at the house and saw his two boys on the couch with their foreheads and noses pressed to the window. "Tell them to come out. I want to talk to them."

Doris signaled to the boys. Walking down the sidewalk, both looked chagrined and nervous as they climbed into the backseat. Walter turned to them. "How are you doing, guys?"

Both chimed, "Fine."

"You know I'm upset that you won't come with me, don't you?"

They nodded.

"It really hurts me." Taking a deep breath, he continued. "I'm going to give your mom my phone number where you can reach me on the road. If you want to talk to me, you'll have to call me. If Bevo Day is more important than me, then that's it. It'll be up to you when you want to call me or see me. Understand?"

Again, both nodded. As Wally, Jr., bit his lower lip, Scotty blinked back his tears. Doris just looked at Walter and shook her head. Then the three of them got out of the car and walked toward the house. Walter slowly drove away. It would be several years before he and his two older sons would have any contact with each other.

Fall, 1975–Winter, 1979. Jimi's overnight incarceration in the St. Charles jail fueled his rebellious nature. His anger toward his father and the law steadily increased. Jim and Sharon blamed the school's environment for their older son's drug dealing. One solution to this problem, they thought, would be a move into the country. So, in 1975, they sold their double-wide mobile home and bought two acres and a house in the rural section of southeast St. Charles County.

It was the American ideal of Smalltown, U.S.A.: woods and fields to roam; a small country church around the bend; neighbors who waved and smiled to everyone, even strangers. But it was not the solution to their son's problem. In 1975 most American public schools still had rampant drug problems leftover from the late 1960's. Their son's new high school was no different.

If Jimi didn't use and deal, he got drunk. Anything for a high. Anything to escape and rebel. His grades dropped to F's. No amount of verbal expletives from a raging father scared him. Not even beatings from his father's hands or his belt or a cord of electrical wire could stop Jimi's defiance.

One day as Jim drove home from work, he noticed a long line of cars and trucks parked up and down the road in front of his house. Close to one hundred teenagers congregated in the yard shouting and drinking. Outside, the stereo blared. Inside the house more teens were spilling their beer and burning holes in the carpet. Jim screamed for them to get out of his house. Then he called the sheriff.

When the police cars arrived, the kids scattered; but the twenty-eight year old man who provided the kegs from the back of his pickup truck was blocked in. Not only did Jim press charges against him, but also fifteen teenagers, including his son, Jimi. This time Sharon pleaded with Jim to put up the fifteen hundred dollar bond money so Jimi wouldn't have to spend the night in jail. She promised her husband she would find a way to get their son straightened out. Jim finally acquiesced. But Jimi's behavior only grew progressively worse. And the arguments between Jim and Sharon intensified.

▪ ▪ ▪

In 1976, Jim went into partnership with another electrician. Two years later he decided to form his own electrical contracting business in St. Charles County. He worked sixteen to eighteen hour days. Although Sharon continued her job as a reservationist with Trans World Airlines, she also kept the electrical company's books and handled all office duties.

Within a year, he had a work crew of ten to fifteen men, and bought five trucks. Because of his numerous connections to city and county officials, and his business contacts with the Jaycees, his company grew. Jim also knew how to talk with anyone, a trait his grandfather taught him as a young boy. People liked him. They thought Jim was friendly and had a good sense of humor. If it weren't for his older son's problems with the law, the Williamses could have been considered an ideal American family.

■ ■ ■

Although many people described JoAnn Calcaterra Notheis as having an impassive demeanor and wary of most people, Toni DiGennaro Molkenbur and JoAnn became the best of friends. Their husbands also formed a steadfast friendship, and the two couples talked and visited together frequently.

When JoAnn was pregnant with the twins, Toni gave her a baby shower. When the twins were christened, Toni and her husband, Tom, were Bryan's godparents. Likewise, when the Molkenbur's had their first child, JoAnn and Walter were the godparents. The two families developed such closeness that one time when Walter and his band performed at Stan and Biggies in Clearwater, Florida, Toni, Tom, JoAnn, and their respective children drove down to visit Walter for a week. During the day they played at the beach; at night they watched Walter on stage. One day they even saw the sights at Disney World together.

JoAnn finally found a woman friend, besides her mother, with whom she could confide in about other people, her husband, her fears, and her problems. After the two young mothers put their children to bed, they would get on the telephone every night for two to three hours and talk about their day. Sometimes JoAnn told Toni about the fights she and Walter would have. JoAnn and Walter had great passion in their relationship, but they were also two strongheaded people, each wanting control of the other. Several times the police knocked on their door and told them to settle down because neighbors had complained of their clamorous arguments.

On several occasions Tom and Toni loaned their friends money to pay taxes, even though Walter would send JoAnn sufficient cash each week. Many times JoAnn would want Toni to shop with her. And often she told Toni about her strong suspicions that Walter was fooling around with other women. If Walter played in St. Louis, JoAnn immediately went to Walter's hotel room after the performance and often saw several women standing outside his door. She would walk up to them and ask, "Who do you think you are waiting for? My husband?" Greg Hoeltzel, the former keyboardist, had seen her pull hair, scratch, hit, whatever it took to let the women who flirted with Walter know that he was not available. She waited a long time to get her man and she didn't want anyone taking him away.

▪ ▪ ▪

Although JoAnn's maiden name of Calcaterra denotes a strong Italian heritage, her mother was full-blooded Irish. JoAnn was not close to her father, but she idolized her mother and had to see her every day. JoAnn's friends said her mother advised her daughter in many areas: how to dress, fix her hair, keep her weight down. If JoAnn began to put on two or three pounds, her mother would tell her to lose it. Mrs. Calcaterra was well-dressed, well-manicured, and exceptionally classy. Probably of all the people JoAnn loved, she loved no other person as she had loved her mother. When doctors diagnosed her mother with cancer, it devastated the entire family, especially, JoAnn. A year later, in 1978, her mother died.

As soon as Toni found out about Mrs. Calcaterra's death, she went over to JoAnn's. JoAnn sat at the kitchen table, her eyes red-rimmed and swollen. When she saw Toni, she clung to her friend as a new wave of tears erupted. Another friend of JoAnn's was there, Judy Steiner. Judy kept talking and comforting JoAnn while Toni cleaned up the kitchen, bathed the twins and put them to bed. When Walter called from out of town to make sure Toni was there to help out, JoAnn and Judy spoke to him. Just as Toni reached for the phone, JoAnn hung up. Despite this seemingly insignificant slight, it began the splintering of Toni and JoAnn's friendship.

With her mother's death, JoAnn's world quickly fractured into a million insecurities. No longer could she see or talk to her mother each day. She was like a black hole, imploding, sucking in all her fears, grief, anger. Many people said they saw a marked change in her when her mother died, even before the funeral. It was as if something in her had also died. Once the mortician embalmed Mrs. Calcaterra, JoAnn would not allow anyone else to touch her mother. She personally dressed her mother, fixed her hair, and applied the make-up.

Kay and Walter, Sr., attended the funeral to pay their respects. Despite her being Walter's wife, JoAnn had told other people that she felt they didn't like her. That night the tension heightened. JoAnn acknowledged her in-laws in a cool, remote manner. When the twins, who were now six years old, approached their paternal grandparents and called them "Grandma and Grandpa," Toni noticed a raging glare in JoAnn's eyes.

After Mr. and Mrs. Notheis left, Toni said she saw JoAnn grab both twins by their hands and yank them out of the room. As Toni followed them to a side room, she saw her friend take the twins by their collars and shove them against the wall.

In a low, menacing voice, she pointed to the visitation room and said, "You have only one grandmother and she's in that box in there. If I ever hear you call them Grandma and Grandpa again, you'll pay for it!"

Toni intervened. "JoAnn, stop it. I know you're upset, but don't say that to the kids."

"Stay out of it, Toni. Just stay the hell out of my business!"

After the funeral, JoAnn severed all ties with Toni and Tom. The twelve years of laughter, tears, and love suddenly ceased. Despite numerous attempts to talk to and visit JoAnn after the funeral, Toni said JoAnn refused to resume their friendship.

■ ■ ■

In the spring of 1979, Walter and JoAnn moved to Park Charles South, a subdivision in St. Charles County. They lived less than five miles from Jim and Sharon Williams.

Spring, 1979–Summer, 1983. When Walter and JoAnn moved to their new house in the Park Charles South subdivision, for a short time they were happy. The house acted as a connecting line between the two, just like a newborn baby temporarily bonds an estranged wife and husband. They reveled in the lovely two-story house, which backed to a ten acre lake. Both felt exceptionally proud of it, as it was indicative of their rise to a higher socio-economic level.

One of the first things they did was register Bryan and Mindy in the Francis Howell School District. The closest school, Fairmount Elementary, was a new school less than a mile from their house. Larry Smith, the former bandleader of the Kommotions, was now the principal at Fairmount. Hearing a familiar voice talking to his secretary, he stepped out of his office and saw JoAnn and Walter with their two children.

When Walter glanced up and saw Larry, he laughed and jokingly said to the secretary, "Never mind! We're going to put our kids into the parochial schools. I know this guy's background!"

Fairmount not only acquired Walter's children as part of the student body, but in a short time, JoAnn began working there as a secretary for the principal in the K-3 section of the school.

▪ ▪ ▪

Walter had a new home but he was rarely there to enjoy it. His bookings took him to many places throughout the country, especially up and down the east coast: Atlantic City, Syracuse, Albany, Rochester, Boston, Philadelphia, the Poconos, Atlanta, and Clearwater, Florida. Several times he played in Las Vegas, singing on the small stages next to the main show. On a few occasions, his agent booked the band to perform in the tourist mecca of Aruba.

For several years, Walter's show had taken on a Las Vegas appearance. He had a voice people loved, and he knew how to work his audiences with light bantering and corny jokes. His musicians were proficient; the selections ranged from popular oldies to current songs, including numbers by Elvis and Neil Diamond; and his dancers were gorgeously sexy. The young women were highly trained, versatile, and scantily clad.

In 1980, one of his dancers left. A tall, slender, twenty year old beauty replaced her. She had long legs, long brunette hair and, despite her energy onstage, she was quiet and soft spoken. Her name: Serina Michaels.

When JoAnn finally met her husband's new dancer, she sensed future trouble. JoAnn was only thirty-four and still very attractive, but she felt threatened by this young girl. Although she had supplanted Doris, Walter's first wife, she didn't want anyone to reciprocate and do the same to her.

JoAnn's figure continued to turn heads, and she was a capable dancer and singer. People who knew about the situation said that JoAnn tried to convince Walter to use her as part of his act. He firmly rejected the idea. Numerous arguments began focusing on Serina. JoAnn wanted her gone. Walter said no.

JoAnn yelled, badgered, cried, but to no avail. Walter remained adamant about keeping Serina as part of his act. The marriage, which by now was already shaky, grew more tumultuous and distrustful.

▪ ▪ ▪

Since childhood, Walter was susceptible to respiratory infections. At least once or twice a year, he would have a bout with pneumonia. The doctors cautioned him to quit smoking, but he ignored their warnings.

Around September of 1980, he was playing at Atlantic City and became ill. His cough worsened and a fever soon followed. Bob and Diana DeAngelis were in the audience one night. They had visited with Walter briefly before his performance and noticed his face looked pasty white and he had a rough, deep cough. Both cautioned him about going on stage that night, but he ignored them. Walter never missed a performance. He had other people relying on him for a paycheck; and if he couldn't perform, the act didn't go on, and no one got paid.

Immediately after his performance, Bob and Diana took Walter to the emergency room of a nearby hospital. The attending physician placed the stethoscope on Walter's chest and back. He listened intently.

"How long have you had this cough and congestion?"

"Just a few days," replied Walter.

"I hear a lot of fluid in your lungs. Even if we didn't take x-rays, this fluid, accompanied by your cough and high fever, indicates that you have pneumonia. And it's not the walking kind either. I want to admit you tonight."

Walter shook his head. "No way, Doc. I have to perform two nights from now. In my business there are no sick days."

"Mr. Notheis, if you don't take care of your health, you may not be around to perform much longer."

"Sorry, but I can't take time off."

The doctor looked exasperated, but he knew he couldn't force Walter to be admitted. "Okay, I'll give you a penicillin shot and a prescription for antibiotics. Get plenty of bed rest between now and your next performance. Drink lots of liquids. And I suggest you quit smoking."

Bob and Diana took Walter back to his room and called JoAnn, telling her that Walter had pneumonia and that he needed someone to take care of him. She assured them she would be on the next flight to Atlantic City.

She stayed for two days, but then she told him she needed to get back to the kids and her job.

"JoAnn, if you leave me right now, I'll never let you travel with me again."

The next morning when JoAnn left, his parents flew up to help nurse him back to health. Shortly after this, Walter and Serina became lovers.

▪ ▪ ▪

Over the next two years, the dissension between Walter and JoAnn increased. JoAnn essentially raised Mindy and Bryan by herself, and she proved to be a caring and loving mother to her two children. She also worked as a full time secretary at the school. When she got home, she had a household to run. There was no husband to share daily concerns with at the dinner table or while lying in bed. There was only the pillow next to her to grab onto during the night. Although married, JoAnn felt trapped. In four years she would be forty years old, middle-aged, and she wondered if she still would be living her life with a man who was seldom home.

When Walter did come home, the twins knew their father expected certain behavior. What they could get by with with their mother, would not be tolerated by their father. He might be somewhat of a local celebrity, but because he usually worked out of town, they lacked the closeness which develops when a parent is consistently in the home to guide and nurture the children.

Since he had hired Serina, whenever Walter returned to St. Louis, the household alternated from heated arguments to icy aloofness. The love Walter and JoAnn once shared so passionately, abated. JoAnn wanted a divorce. She wanted to feel loved again. But Walter refused to discuss either a divorce or Serina, except to continually deny any involvement with his dancer. He did not want to relive the psychological trauma of another divorce.

▪ ▪ ▪

After JoAnn's mother died, her father, John Calcaterra, lived alone. Although JoAnn wasn't especially close to her father, Walter wanted John to move in with them. He checked with various building contractors on how much it would cost to build an apartment downstairs for his father-in-law. The house already had a walk-out basement. If they added a fully equipped kitchen, full bath, living room, and bedroom, John would have his privacy. After getting several bids, they selected a general contractor and the building began.

In October of 1982, Jim Williams pulled up to #30 Pershing Lake Drive. JoAnn was in the driveway washing the car. When Jim walked towards her, he noticed goosebumps and red splotches on her bare legs.

"Hey, kinda cool to be doing that, isn't it?"

JoAnn looked up and saw a tall, robust man with thick dark hair approaching her.

"Hi, my name's Jim Williams. I'm the electrical contractor here to do some work on your place. You must be Mrs. Notheis."

"Yeah, but call me JoAnn." Placing the soapy sponge back in the water, she wiped her hands on a nearby towel and shook his hand. "Let me show you in."

From the first moment he saw JoAnn, Jim was attracted to

her sultry Sophia Loren looks. He also thought she had a lot of class, and found her easy to talk to. Before long, they had established a friendship. JoAnn would tell him about herself, her marriage, and Jim would do likewise. As they developed a closeness, they became lovers.

■ ■ ■

For the next several months, Jim plied JoAnn with flowers and books of poetry. He'd either have them sent directly to her office at the school, or place them on the front seat of her car. Since Walter had been so preoccupied with his singing career and his new dancer, JoAnn had almost forgotten what it felt like to be desirable. And Jim did his best to make her feel like a beautiful woman again.

Being in love with JoAnn detracted from the love Jim felt for Sharon. He was no longer nineteen. He was in his early forties and had not felt deep passion in years. Except on rare occasions, his ordinary married life tended to banish strong sexual desires for Sharon. This new forbidden love heightened his yearning, but created havoc at home. Jim's younger son, Brett, noticed that the fights between his mom and dad became routine battles.

Sharon found out about his female 'friend.' "You and this JoAnn are getting kind of close, aren't you?"

"We're just friends."

She looked at Jim, her hands on her hips. "You talk to her more than you do me. What's going on between you two?"

"Nothin'. We're just friends. No big deal. She's like a sister I never had, that's all."

"I think it's more, and I want you to stop seeing her. Understand?"

"Damnit!" shouted Jim. "No way you or anyone else is going to tell me who I can or cannot have as a friend." Pointing his finger in Sharon's face, he growled, "Now, do you understand."

Sometimes the arguments ended with Jim shaking her. Other times, Jim's rage consumed him, and a few of Sharon's co-workers at Trans World Airlines said she would come to work with bruises or a black eye.

Although Jim had told his son, Brett, that he had considered divorcing Sharon, he also added that he had too much money invested in the electrical business, and that Sharon would probably try to take everything he had worked so hard to attain.

▪ ▪ ▪

Because Walter spent most of his time away from St. Louis, he was like a stranger to his children. When Jim spent several weeks at the Notheis home doing the electrical work, he said Bryan followed him around like a magnet. Jim liked kids. And he noticed ten year old Bryan was ravenous for male attention. He showed Walter's son how to install electrical outlets and splice wires. He also talked about hunting and fishing and camping out, none of which Bryan had been exposed to. By the end of the three weeks that it took to finish the job, Jim had become an important influence on the boy.

In late January, 1983, Bryan's baseball team needed a sponsor. When he asked his mother if he could call Jim to ask him to be the sponsor, she thought it would be okay. Jim agreed, and Bryan was ecstatic.

The season began in April and ran through to July. Jim attended most practices and games. And the bonding between Walter's son and Jim deepened to a surrogate father-son relationship. Gradually, Jim's importance penetrated the Notheis household.

Once, when Walter spent a couple of weeks singing in a St. Louis club, he briefly attended one of Bryan's games and finally met the man who would shortly be moving into his home and heading his household. As Bryan went up to bat, Jim could tell he was nervous because he wanted to impress his father.

Each time the ball came his way, he swung, whether it was too high, too low, or right down the middle. He struck out. When he walked back to the bench, his head drooped and his shoulders slumped.

Jim walked over to Bryan. "Hey, bud, don't worry. It happens to even the greatest ballplayers."

About this time, Walter walked over. "What happened, son? I think you better start lifting some iron." Giving Bryan a tap on his shoulder, he said, "Gotta get to the job. See you tomorrow."

■ ■ ■

As the months passed, Jim saw JoAnn every opportunity he could. When Walter performed out of town, they would meet at Bruce Schone's Automotive, leave one car there and take off together. Sometimes he would park his car at a neighbor of JoAnn's, "Doc" Spraul's, and bring her bags of vegetables from his garden.

Jim loved JoAnn's deep, rich voice and her subtle intelligence. They discussed their respective marital problems. She told Jim that before she had met him she had asked Walter for a divorce. Walter had responded, "Hell, no! There's never going to be a divorce. The only way you're getting out of this marriage is in a pine box."

Walter was expected home for one week the latter part of August, 1983, and a couple of times in September and October. Jim felt desperate about not being able to see JoAnn when Walter returned. He wanted her for himself.

■ ■ ■

One day in July, Jim worked at an electrical job with two of his employees, Chris Henson and Don Matley. Henson anchored switch boxes in the wall next to Jim, while Matley connected white and black wires to the terminal across the room.

Jim had his head down, concentrating on the wires, when he asked Chris, "Do you know of any hit men?"

Henson's eyes widened as he glanced over at Matley, who had also heard Jim's question. "Well, no, but do you have a job that needs to be done?" Henson had thought his boss was joking, but there was no laughter, not even a hint of jesting coming from his normally congenial employer.

"There's this guy that works out of state who's abusive to his wife and kids. I think he might be in Minnesota. Anyway, I want to find someone to take care of him. You know, make it look like an accident."

"I don't know any hit men, Jim."

"Well, do me a favor and check around. I'll pay five thousand cash to have him eliminated. But it's gotta look like an accident. Hear?"

"Sure. I'll keep my ears open."

Shortly after the conversation, Jim left to check on other electrical jobs he had going on in St. Charles, and Henson and Matley discussed Jim's request. At first they thought he was kidding, but then they believed he might have been serious. Not until three and a half years later did Matley call Henson to again discuss Jim's inquiry about a hit man. Yet neither contacted the police.

▪ ▪ ▪

In late August, 1983, Walter came off the road for a week to celebrate his father's retirement party, which was held at a banquet room of Orlando Gardens in south St. Louis County. Close to sixty people attended and Walter gave one of the many toasts, praising his father's fine character. During the party, Walter's brother, Ronnie, invited Walter, JoAnn, and the twins to come out to a clubhouse that he and his wife had rented for a week by the river. Ronnie owned a boat and several pairs of waterskis. Walter thought it would be fun, and said they'd come out late the next morning.

The day was typical of August in St. Louis: hot and muggy. A perfect Sunday to be on the Mississippi. But as soon as Walter and his family pulled in front of the clubhouse, Ronnie and his wife, also named Joanne, sensed the tension. Walter and JoAnn chatted with everyone except each other. All day, not one word was exchanged between them. The families cruised up and down the river, occasionally putting in at one of the many sandy, manmade islands jutting out of the muddy water. The kids laughed when Ronnie lost his balance and plunged into the boat's wake. But the laughter between the adults was forced because of the animosity Walter and JoAnn exuded in their silent anger.

Once they all returned to the clubhouse, Ronnie and Walter barbecued chicken, hamburgers, and hot dogs. Ronnie's wife, an attractive, articulate woman, went upstairs to the kitchen to prepare baked beans, potato salad, and corn on the cob. As she was shucking the corn, JoAnn came in.

"Is there anything I can help you with?

"Sure, how about slicing some onions to put on the hamburgers."

When JoAnn first married Walter, she seemed nice, but she never allowed anyone in the family to get too close to her. She told Ronnie that she didn't like Walter to talk on the phone so much to Kay. At the same time, she thought it was all right to see her own mother every day, and when she couldn't visit, to at least talk to her on the phone. She also felt Walter's family never fully accepted her because of the affair and the traumatic divorce which followed. Although Ronnie's wife had previously tried to warm up to JoAnn, JoAnn maintained her civil wall. However, today JoAnn revealed some of her feelings to her sister-in-law.

"I'm sure you notice Walter and me not talking to each other."

"Yes, it's a bit obvious."

JoAnn looked at her sister-in-law and let out a sigh. "When Walter and I first got married, I got used to being alone most of the time. But, now I'm tired of it. I know I'll never have a normal marriage with him. And, to tell you the truth, I don't have feelings for Walter anymore. At this point, I'm not sure what to do about it."

"If you're that miserable, leave him."

"I've thought about it, a lot, but he won't talk about a divorce."

"I don't know what to tell you, JoAnn."

The conversation soon ended and JoAnn went downstairs and sat by herself next to the water.

September–October, 1983. Bob Kuban hosted a cable show on Saturdays, featuring various musicians and singers in the St. Louis area. During the winter of 1983, he interviewed Walter Scott. When Walter arrived half an hour early for the taping, Kuban's surprised look caused Walter to laugh. "Yeah, a lot of things changed when I got my own band. Now I'm the one who gets upset when one of my musicians is late!"

After the interview, they reminisced about the national success that Kuban and Walter achieved in the mid-60's. Both concluded that it would be a neat idea to have all the former members get together to play the popular songs during that era in a reunion concert.

Over the summer, Kuban called the former band members, the Fox Theater, and several promoters. All acknowledged the concert would generate a lot of interest in St. Louis, especially with the baby boomers who followed Walter Scott and the Kuban band around the St. Louis area in the 1960's. Once Budweiser agreed to sponsor the concert, the date was set for June 23, 1984, with the first rehearsal scheduled for October.

▪ ▪ ▪

In late September, 1983, Walter came back to St. Louis for a week. He and JoAnn went over to Kuban's house to discuss further details about the impending concert.

When they got to Kuban's, they all went downstairs by the bar to talk. Walter, Kuban, and Kuban's girlfriend, Juanita, sat at one end of the bar sipping soda. JoAnn, more quiet than usual, sat on a stool at the far end of the bar, staring in their direction, but saying nothing.

They talked about what songs should be included in the concert, how they would dress, different lighting effects, and what group to use as an opener. The two men, now middle-aged, became excited about bringing the past back to St. Louis.

"Walter, you know what's going to happen if this thing comes off?"

"Yeah, it could mean big-time again."

"I was thinking the same thing. And, if we could get another hit record going, well, shit, we'd be getting concert bookings across the country." Kuban hesitated a moment. "Listen, if this concert does generate a resurgence for us, you can take the band out on the road, handle the monies, whatever you want. I've got enough things going on back here. If you'd want me to make some guest appearances with you, great, but no way I want to go back on the road."

Walter glanced up at JoAnn, who remained stoic, then turned to Kuban. "I wouldn't mind working the concerts out of town; but to tell you the truth, I'm getting too old for this constant shit of always being gone. I'm ready to get off the road."

JoAnn raised an eyebrow and sat up a little straighter. Before she had severed her friendship with Toni, JoAnn told her that Walter had occasionally mentioned getting off the road to become a booking agent. She told him, "You made me a part-time wife, and I got used to it. There's no way I could be a full-time wife, so forget the idea."

Kuban sensed the silent exchange between Walter and JoAnn, but let it pass.

After discussing the concert for another fifteen or twenty minutes, JoAnn suddenly spoke up. In her husky voice, she said, "I think each of you should take out a hundred thousand dollar insurance policy, naming the other as beneficiary."

Kuban looked quizzically at her. "What in the hell are you talking about?"

"Suppose something happens. If one of you doesn't show up, then the whole thing goes down and we all lose a lot of money."

"JoAnn, that's ludicrous! Where am I going? Shit, I've never had a life insurance policy on myself. And, why should I have Walter as my beneficiary and me his?"

"You may have something else booked near the concert date and not be able to make it back in time."

"This is crazy! Let me show you my schedule of bookings for next summer." As Kuban headed upstairs to his office, he wondered why Walter had suddenly gotten quiet when JoAnn unveiled her idea.

Returning, he sat next to JoAnn and opened his 1984 calendar book. "Okay, see, here I am in June. I play a few dances at the beginning of the month. Then the week before the reunion concert, I'm in Chicago for a wedding reception. I have a booking the end of June. But, look here, JoAnn, there's nothing for four days before or four days after the concert. So, no problem."

JoAnn said, "Whatever," and resumed her reticence.

Kuban noticed Walter still hadn't reacted to his wife's request. Shortly after the conversation, they left.

After they had gone, Kuban turned to his girlfriend and said, "Something's up. I wonder what that was all about."

▪ ▪ ▪

For the first time in seventeen years, all the original members of Bob Kuban and the In-Men got together at Spatz Lounge for their first practice session in early October, 1983. Some flew into St. Louis from Las Vegas, Atlanta, and Indianapolis. When Greg Hoeltzel, now a successful orthodontist in a prestigious section of St. Louis County, knocked at the locked door of the lounge, Walter opened it. They exchanged big smiles and hearty handshakes. Everyone joked, laughed, and cut up for the first thirty minutes.

As they started practicing, several of the members struggled with the right chords and notes. But after a few attempts, everyone started playing in sync. Even the same jokes and the same dance steps they used to do in their routine seventeen years earlier came together. During the practice of "The Cheater," no one in the band missed a note.

JoAnn stopped by with the twins. She had on a jacket with "Walter Scott" emblazoned across its back. Despite the growing tension between them, JoAnn still liked to be known as Walter Scott's wife. For a short time she chatted with a couple of the band members, their wives and girlfriends.

Before Walter left practice that Sunday afternoon in October, he set a date to meet with Mike Krenski during his Christmas break home to discuss further details about the concert and possible new songs for his band.

It was the last time any of the former members of Bob Kuban and the In-Men would see Walter.

October 19, 1983. The day had been stormy with torrential rains, lightning, and strong winds, but by six-thirty in the evening the unsettling weather had moved eastward. Jim and Sharon just returned from eating dinner at a local St. Charles restaurant. A few minutes later Alice Almaroad, Sharon's mother, called from Marion, Illinois. Sharon told her mother she planned going to the Wednesday night church service at Harvester Baptist Church on Highway 94 South. She had been attending a church in St. Louis but wanted to find one closer to home. When Alice asked if Jim would also be going, Sharon said no, that he would probably stay home and watch television.

▪ ▪ ▪

Around seven-twenty, Joe Dingledine and his wife were heading southwest on Central School Road in St. Charles County when they saw the red glare of taillights sticking out of a ditch close to the beginning of a bridge. Dingledine stopped his car and got out. The steep incline led to a creek. Sliding down the wet grass, he noticed the driver's door wide open and saw a small foot-high fire in the grass next to it. No one was around. After stomping it out, he ran back up the hill and shouted to his wife to call for help. Then back down he went.

The 1982 yellow Cadillac Coupe DeVille's engine was still running, the back tires spewing small flecks of mud up in the air. Dingledine climbed into the driver's side. Because the seat was as far back as it could go, he had to sit on the edge to turn off the key. Suddenly, he heard a loud, rough gasp. Looking down, he noticed a woman's body jammed under the dash on the passenger side. Once more he hurried up the embankment to flag someone down.

At seven-thirty, Officer Ed Copeland of the St. Charles County Sheriff's Department sat in his squad car at the entrance of the Park Charles South subdivision when he heard a call from someone's CB about the accident. Twenty seconds later the dispatcher reported the incident on his police radio. With siren blaring and lights flashing, Copeland arrived on the scene in less than three minutes from the initial report.

When he pulled up behind Dingledine's car, he quickly got out and rushed down the hill. Copeland climbed into the Cadillac on the driver's side, and he too heard the woman desperately wheezing for air. Placing one hand behind her head and the other on her forehead, he opened her airway wider and she began to breathe a little easier. The young policeman noticed that the back of her head felt soft, wet, mushy, resembling the consistency of jelly. Yet the blood had also started to coagulate. Why would this occur, he wondered, if the accident just happened? He made a mental note about this incongruity.

Within a few minutes, the Cottleville Volunteer Fire Department arrived and an assistant chief, Ed Litteken, slid down the hill to assist Officer Copeland. Litteken noticed that the woman's hair looked partially off her head. Realizing it was a long, blond wig, he took it off and threw it into the back seat. He saw a bowling ball bag and tossed that also in the back. Another member of the fire department, Rich Podhorn, soon joined Litteken.

Podhorn went around to the passenger side. When he opened the door, an overwhelming odor of gasoline permeated the air. "Open gas," he shouted.

A paramedic, Jeff Keller, followed Podhorn down the hill, and another paramedic brought down the Stokes basket. When Keller placed his hand on the back of the woman's head, he too noticed its pulpy texture. Once they got the woman in the basket and up the hill, they transferred her onto a stretcher and placed her in the ambulance.

Podhorn and Keller cut off her clothes and put trauma pants on her. The smell of gasoline overpowered them, and blood slowly dripped from the back of the woman's head, creating bright red splotches on Keller's shoes and the floor of the ambulance.

While the paramedics had been working on the woman in the car, Officer Copeland radioed headquarters and requested a photo ID unit to come to the scene. Twenty minutes later, no one showed. He placed another call. The dispatcher informed him that his supervisory officer had instead sent the unit to divert traffic away from the accident. Therefore, no pictures would be taken of the actual scene.

▪ ▪ ▪

Meanwhile, the owner of the vehicle had been identified and a call was placed at eight o'clock to the Williams's residence.

"Mr. James Williams, please."

"Speaking."

"Are you the owner of a 1982 yellow Cadillac Coupe DeVille?"

"Sure am."

"The woman in the car has been in an accident on Central School Road."

"What? Sharon's been hurt?"

"We've taken her to St. Joseph's Hospital, sir. If you stay where you are, we'll have a car come by to pick you up."

"Uh, sure. Is she okay?"

"Can't tell, sir."

▪ ▪ ▪

At the hospital, three physicians worked on Sharon. After she had a CAT scan and an EEG taken, they transferred her to the Intensive Care Unit. Because of the powerful gasoline fumes, Nurse Lynn Behrens began to bathe Sharon.

Right away she noticed a general redness covered Sharon's entire body. As Behrens started to wash her, the nurse's hands and arms up to the elbow began to tingle, then burn. She and an aid put on long rubber gloves, but they didn't help much. As they gently rubbed the wash cloth over Sharon's body, the top layer of skin came off around the groin, the folds of the arms, and under her breasts. In her report, she indicated that these areas looked a mean raw-red.

After washing Sharon, they placed her on a ventilator, then hooked multiple IV drugs into her veins to keep her kidneys, lungs, heart, and blood pressure going.

▪ ▪ ▪

Jim's younger son, Brett, arrived at the hospital with his fiance, Jan, shortly after he had been notificed about his mother's accident. Because Jim's older son, Jimi, was serving time in a Florida penitentiary, he was unable to be at his mother's bedside with the rest of his family. Around midnight, Sharon's mother received a call about her daughter's accident. She and a niece, Imogene Benton, left Marion, Illinois, immediately and arrived at St. Joseph's Hospital around two-thirty in the morning.

Sharon's family members and friends stood vigil in the waiting room next to the intensive care unit, crying and comforting one another. Brett was perplexed when the doctor told him that his mother had been found under the dash on the passenger side of the car. Everytime she got in a car, whether as a driver or a passenger, she was adamant about wearing a seatbelt. She never turned the ignition key until it was secured.

■ ■ ■

October 20, 1983. Around ten o'clock the next morning, Dr. Wipfler, a surgeon at the hospital, took Jim aside. "Mr. Williams, it doesn't look good for your wife. As I told you last night, she has swelling of the brain from the injuries she sustained to the back of her head. The CAT scan and EEG tests indicate that your wife is brain dead."

Jim began to cry. "Is there any hope at all?"

"No, sir. None. I'm sorry, but I need your permission to unhook the life support functions."

Jim and Brett talked briefly about the decision. Both agreed. Once Jim consented, a representative from Washington University in St. Louis asked if he would consider donating Sharon's organs and bone marrow to the university. Again, he acquiesced.

At eleven-thirty in the morning on October 20, 1983, the doctors disconnected the life support systems and Sharon Elaine Williams, Jim's wife of twenty-five years, died. The death certificate stated the cause of death: cranial cerebral trauma. No autopsy was performed.

■ ■ ■

Later, when Officer Copeland returned to headquarters, one of the paramedics was also making out his report. Both men voiced their suspicions that for this type of minor accident, Sharon Williams should have sustained some injuries to the front of her head, not the back. And certainly not of the severity they witnessed. Copeland spoke to his commander about his suspicions.

No investigation followed.

Nurse Lynn Behrens and one of the physicians also expressed strong opinions that something was not right. The type of accident Sharon had experienced appeared inconsistent with her critical condition. Later, more of the medical personnel who worked on Sharon also quietly spoke about their suspicions, but no follow-up transpired. A doctor later placed a call to the Sheriff's office. When the dispatcher put him on hold for a lengthy period of time, he hung up and never called again.

▪ ▪ ▪

October 21–22, 1983. After spending the night at Jim's house, Sharon's mother and her niece woke up early Friday morning and drove back home to Marion. Jim, Brett, Brett's fiance, and an employee of Jim's, Dennis Carver, soon followed in two separate vehicles.

Jim, Alice, and Brett discussed funeral arrangements with Larry Hughes, the funeral home director. Visitation was that evening from five until nine. Family members, friends, and acquaintances cried, hugged, and shook their heads over Sharon's quick demise. The next afternoon Sharon's casket was lowered into her grave at Fountain Cemetery.

Alice walked up to Jim and placed her hand on his arm. "Jim, you are coming back to my house for the funeral reception, aren't you?"

Jim took a deep breath. "No, don't think I will. I have my own home to go back to."

"But everyone will be there. All the neighbors brought over dishes of food."

"I'm not in the mood for it. All last night and today I've heard all I want to hear about this whole thing. I'm tired and heading home."

Before leaving Marion, Jim told Brett he needed to go back

to the funeral home and load up some plants to take back to St. Charles. While Brett and Dennis Carver placed the plants in the vehicles, Jim told Brett he had to make a telephone call and headed up the stairs.

When he returned, he said, "Brett, I want you to ride back with me. Jan can go with Dennis. I want to talk to you." Turning to Brett's fiance, he asked, "You don't mind, do you, Jan?"

She looked at him quizzically, but said, "No."

As they proceeded back to St. Charles, Jim and Brett discussed Sharon, the funeral, and Jim's future. Then Jim began talking about JoAnn. "You know I've been seeing JoAnn. And we're really close. Your mother was a beautiful lady but she's gone, and I need to keep going on. I can't dwell on the past."

Brett nodded.

"I really care for JoAnn and I'd like to build a life with her and her kids."

The conversation switched to other areas for the remainder of the trip, but Brett kept thinking it was strange that less than two hours ago they had buried his mother and now his dad talked about marrying someone who was already married.

When they pulled up to the house, the garage door was closed. After parking the car in the driveway, Jim and Brett walked through the side door of the garage. Immediately, Brett saw JoAnn's Lincoln Town car and wondered what it was doing there. As they entered the kitchen, JoAnn sat at the kitchen table petting Jim's dachshund.

"I brought Fred back."

■ ■ ■

A few days later, Brett stopped by his dad's house late in the afternoon. When he pulled up to the house, he saw JoAnn's car in the driveway. As he entered the back door, silence permeated the rooms. No voices talking. No TV or radio blaring.

Walking through the kitchen, Brett started hollering, "Hey, Dad, where are you?" No response. Going into the living room, he shouted again.

A moment later, Jim opened up the bedroom door, tying his robe together, and shut the door behind him.

"I just stopped by to see how it's going."

"Fine. Just fine. Getting some rest. Really worn out. But otherwise, making it. How about you?"

"Okay. I still can't believe what happened to Mom. Listen, Jan and I wanted to see if you'd like to come over later and have dinner with us."

"Naw. Think I'll take a raincheck on that."

"All right. Well, I'd better get going. See you on the job tomorrow."

▪ ▪ ▪

October 31, 1983. Nine days after Sharon's funeral, Jim no longer concealed his relationship with JoAnn Notheis. Several people had seen them out together. Later, in a police report, Brett said his father called him on Halloween to invite him and Jan to go out with him, JoAnn, and the twins. At dinner, Brett glanced at a bracelet that JoAnn was wearing. It looked familiar. Suddenly, he realized where he had seen it before. On his mother's wrist.

November–December 24, 1983. For several weeks after Sharon's death, Jim and Alice Almaroad, Sharon's mother, called one another frequently. Although he had a florist place flowers on Sharon's grave each week the first year after her demise, he left it up to his mother-in-law to manage matters pertaining to finalizing his wife's burial. During one of the conversations, Alice asked Jim if he was coming back to Marion to pick out a headstone for Sharon.

"Mom, I'm really busy here. Lots of jobs and lots around here to take care of. How about you picking something out?"

"Well, she was your wife for over twenty-five years. Don't you think you should be the one to get it?"

"I wish I could take time off, but can't. You've got the time. Just pick a large enough headstone for Sharon and me."

"All right, if that's how you want to handle it. What do you want written on it?"

"For me, just Jim. You know, J-i-m."

"What about an inscription?"

"Nothing for me."

Alice hesitated, then asked, "I meant on Sharon's side. How about if I put 'Precious Lord, take my hand'?"

"That's fine, Mom. Put anything you think Sharon would have liked. By the way, when are you coming back here to go through her things?"

"I was thinkin' about next week, if that..." Alice began crying over the phone.

"Now listen here. I don't want you crying when you visit me. We've had enough tears and I don't want to see no more. You can come up and pick out anything of Sharon's you want. What you don't want, I'm giving away."

The following week, Alice spent a couple of days at Jim's going through Sharon's clothes, ceramics, sewing equipment, and other personal items. Although she cried when she first walked through the front door, Jim admonished her again for her tears. After that, she did her crying out of his sight.

■ ■ ■

Many of JoAnn's neighbors knew about the affair between her and Jim. For a short time Claudia Brown lived with her in-laws next door to JoAnn, and they became good friends. JoAnn told her about the flowers, poetry books, and clothing Jim gave her throughout the past year. Even the assistant principal, Gary Schisler, and JoAnn's co-worker, Regina Nevvatel, had seen Jim stop by Fairmount Primary to briefly visit JoAnn. Sometimes she'd find a gift in her car when she came out of school after work; other times, she'd get a present from him personally. A day or two before Walter was due home, JoAnn would take them over to one of her neighbors so he wouldn't become suspicious and start asking questions.

In November, JoAnn told Claudia that she was dreading Walter coming home in December. He would have only a couple of days playing a New Year's Eve celebration at the Poconos in Pennsylvania, then he'd be back in St. Louis performing for nine weeks at the Playboy Club and the Hoffman House. During his time home, it would be difficult to see Jim.

"JoAnn, if you love Jim that much, why don't you just get a divorce from Walter?"

"I'd like to, but I know he won't give me one. A few times in the past I've mentioned it and he told me under no circumstances would he even consider it. His first divorce was hell for him, and he vowed never again. Everyone who knows Walter, including his family, will tell you he'll never give me a divorce, no matter how shitty our marriage is."

JoAnn shrugged her shoulders before continuing. "Besides, Jim told me not to worry, that he has a plan."

"Plan? What kind of plan?"

"I have no idea. He just said he'd take care of it."

▪ ▪ ▪

Now that John Calcaterra lived with his daughter and son-in-law, he also saw a lot of Jim. They usually got along fine, but one time they got into an argument.

One day John and Jim were in the kitchen. John, also a large man, looked at Jim and stated, "I think you're intruding by coming over here when Walter's not home. What's going on between you and my daughter?"

"Nothin'. JoAnn and I are friends, just friends, nothin' more."

Jim said that John continued to look him hard in the eyes. "Bull shit! Everytime Walter leaves, you come hightailing it over here. You take JoAnn and the kids out to eat, buy them gifts. Something's not right."

"It's like I told you, we're just friends."

"Well, when Walter comes home at Christmas, I'm going to have a talk with him and we'll see about this."

■ ■ ■

In November, Walter's band played in Albany, New York, at the Turf Inn. Because it would be one of his last performances in the Catskill Mountains for a few months, he called his good friends, Bob and Diana DeAngelis, to join him for dinner before his performance. He also asked if they'd mind Serina joining them. Although Bob and Diana had met Serina when she started dancing in Walter's band, they had never seen her with Walter socially. The first time they saw her, they were shocked. They said she strongly resembled JoAnn when JoAnn was in her early twenties, except Serina's face and demeanor were soft and vulnerable. Something they had never seen in JoAnn's.

During dinner she spoke in her quiet manner, her face glowing each time she met Walter's eyes. One time she accidentally called Walter "Bear" and turned a bright red. Diana kept thinking of Serina's age, twenty-three. She hoped she wouldn't get hurt by being in a relationship with Walter.

Bob had noticed during dinner that despite a lot of smiles and corny jokes from Walter, his friend's right eye twitched and behind the eyes lurked a trace of fear. Bob sensed something was not right. Diana agreed.

■ ■ ■

Walter began his show with a wide range of songs, starting out with "Sugar Pie, Honey Bunch," "Earth Angel," "Ain't No Mountain High Enough," and then to the song which gave him national recognition, "The Cheater." After singing several Neil Diamond hits, he went on break.

When he returned, he took off his tie, pulled his collar high up on the back of his neck and began his Elvis Presley routine. The audience shouted, clapped, and whistled. If they had closed their eyes, they would have sworn it was "the King." In between songs, Walter bantered with the people and told his jokes.

As Walter began his last number for the evening, the furrow between his eyebrows returned. It was a new song which he had just added to his show: "There's a Stranger in My House."

Afterwards, Diana went up to the hotel room to go to sleep while Bob and Walter stayed up most of the night in Walter's room, drinking coffee and talking. Walter's cautiousness would not allow him to get too close to anyone. It had taken some time before he trusted Bob to be candid and reveal his feelings about things, especially his marriage to JoAnn. As they talked into the early morning hours, he told Bob that things weren't right between him and JoAnn, that something was up and he wasn't quite sure what it was. He had a feeling that she was involved in an affair. Bob then recalled the last song Walter had added to his show. It then made sense. Most of Walter's songs hinted at what was going on in his life. They acted as clues that in a normal conversation he refused to disclose.

Walter also told Bob that JoAnn strongly suspected he was having an affair with Serina. He said one night when he was out of his room, the phone rang. Serina and the other dancer had an adjoining room to his. When Serina heard the phone ring, she dashed in to answer it. It was JoAnn. Walter voiced concern about how she would retaliate.

Throughout the remainder of November until he flew back to St. Louis for the Christmas holidays, Walter called Bob and Diana several times a week to let them know his whereabouts. On December 18, 1983, Walter called Bob, who was in the hospital recuperating from an operation. They spoke for close to an hour and agreed to get together soon. They never did.

▪ ▪ ▪

The first week in December, one of Sharon's co-workers at TWA called Jim about some problem she was having with her automobile. For ten years, she had been friends with both Sharon and Jim. Jim told her to come by the next night and he would take a look at it.

When Gretchen Brown arrived, he fixed her car and then they went into the house for a dinner he had prepared. While they finished off a bottle of wine, he talked about JoAnn and said he was in love with her. Later, he took Gretchen upstairs to one of the bedrooms. As he opened the closet door, she saw a long row of brand-new clothes, the tags still attached to the sleeves. "These are JoAnn's Christmas presents."

After they returned to the kitchen, he then turned the conversation to Walter. "That son-of-a-bitch she's married to is an entertainer. He doesn't give a damn about anyone but himself. When he's home, he's abusive to his family. I also hear he's involved in drugs and gambling."

"Why does she stay with him?"

"Who knows? But maybe not for long. Someday something's going to happen to that son-of-a-bitch."

A few days later, Jim called Gretchen at work. "Hey, Gretchen, I want you to do me a favor. Check the flights coming in from Harrisburg, Pennsylvania, around December 18 or 19. See which flight Walter Scott is coming in on."

"Sure. Just don't tell anyone. I'm not supposed to do this."

"No problem."

▪ ▪ ▪

When Walter left the Poconos for a short period of time, he stored the instruments and costumes in his trailer, leaving it at the home of Frank Floto of Mechanicsburg, Pennsylvania. Floto also drove Walter to the airport on December 19. Lately, he had noticed Walter looking depressed. Once, Walter told Floto that he didn't feel like performing anymore but he had a family to support, plus he had to pay child support for his first two sons, and he owed the IRS.

Walter placed a call to JoAnn, telling her when to pick him up at Lambert Field, also known as the St. Louis International Airport. When he got off the phone, he was visibly upset.

"What's up?" asked Floto.

Walter's face flushed. "Damnit. JoAnn said she may not be there. Said something's wrong with the car's battery. If you ask me, it sounds like she doesn't want me home for the next nine weeks."

Although JoAnn was late, she did borrow her father's car to pick up Walter in the afternoon on the nineteenth. She dropped him off, telling him her bowling league was expecting her. Around seven she returned and fixed dinner. The rest of the evening, the family sat together watching television.

■ ■ ■

For the next couple of days, it was quiet around the Notheis home. JoAnn went to work; the kids, to school. Only Walter and John remained home together during the day. The only time Walter left was to visit his dentist, who told him he had periodontal disease. The next day he was scheduled for a treatment, but a heavy snowstorm dumped eight inches on the St. Louis area, closing schools and some small businesses. Since his dentist canceled all office appointments, Walter spent several hours with his snowblower cleaning off his and the neighbors' driveways.

Around noon on December 22, 1983, he visited a few people, including his mother and both grandmothers. Ever since he had divorced Doris and married JoAnn, his Grandma Notheis, an orthodox Catholic, had refused to speak to him. On this particular day, fourteen years later, she welcomed her grandson with hugs and kisses. They mended the rift. He also picked up fourteen one hundred dollar bills from his father. The week before, he sent his parents a cashier's check for over four thousand dollars. Most of it was to repay his parents for a past loan. That evening he went by himself to the Chesterfield Mall to do his Christmas shopping.

The next night before he left the house to meet with Bill Garvey and Bob Burns, owners of Spatz Lounge, about the reunion concert, Walter told JoAnn, "If I decide to check out tonight, your Christmas present is in the closet."

He got to the lounge around ten in the evening. After talking about the concert, the three of them went to a party nearby. The host had a parakeet in a cage. Both Garvey and Burns said Walter kept staring at the bird. He then turned to them and said, "Wouldn't it be nice just to up and fly away sometime?"

Walter got home at three-thirty the next morning, nothing unusual for his lifestyle. After sleeping late into the next morning, he spent the rest of the day with his family.

■ ■ ■

Many of the neighbors in Park Charles South said that Walter appeared exceptionally wary and nervous on this trip home. He had every reason to be anxious. Several neighbors later made police statements that they had frequently seen Jim Williams parked in front of their homes observing the Notheis' residence.

Besides Walter being watched by JoAnn's lover, the family began receiving numerous strange phone calls. As soon as one of them answered the phone, the caller would hang up. One time Mindy answered and a menacing voice said, "Walter's dead. Walter's dead."

Kay and ten month old Walter maintained a close bond throughout his life.

The Notheis family in the late 1940's. Ronnie in Kay's arms, Walter, Sr., and young Walter.

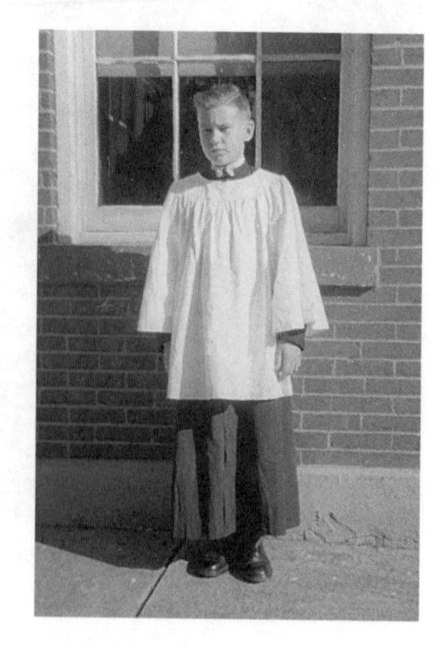

Twelve year old Walter as an altar boy.

Walter's senior picture at St. Mary's High School

Bob Kuban and The In-Men, 1965. Left to right: Pat Hixon, trumpet; Harry Simon, sax; head peeking behind guitarist is Skip Weisser, trombone; guitarist was sitting in for Ray Schulte, name unknown; Bob Kuban, drums; Walter Scott, lead singer (next to Bob); Mike Krenski, bass; and Greg Hoeltzel, keyboard.

Mel Friedman, manager, at Technisonic Studios.

Walter recording 'Just You Wait' at Columbia Studios.

Hamming it up in Nashville. Mike Krenski, Ray Schulte, Walter, and Terry Schieler holding Greg Hoeltzel.

A happy moment in their shaky marriage in 1968. Doris, Ronnie, Walter with Wally, Jr. and Scotty.

In 1969 at McKendree College in Lebanon, IL. Bob DeAngelis (l), Walter Scott, and president of Plato Fraternity, Bob Smith.

In 1983, the middle-aged musicians practicing for their reunion concert, which never took place. Left to right: Pat Hixon, Harry Simon, Skip Weisser, Ray Schulte, Bob Kuban, Walter, Mike Krenski, and Greg Hoeltzel.

Jim Williams in his office prior to his arrest.

Lt. Wes Simcox of the St. Charles County Sheriff's office directed the nine year investigation.

Police, Dr. Mary Case, and members of the Cottleville Fire Department retrieving Walter's body from the cistern.

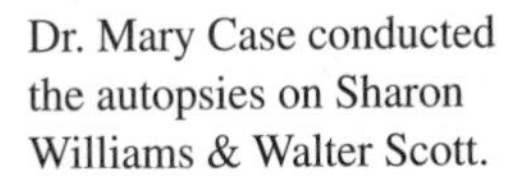

Dr. Mary Case conducted the autopsies on Sharon Williams & Walter Scott.

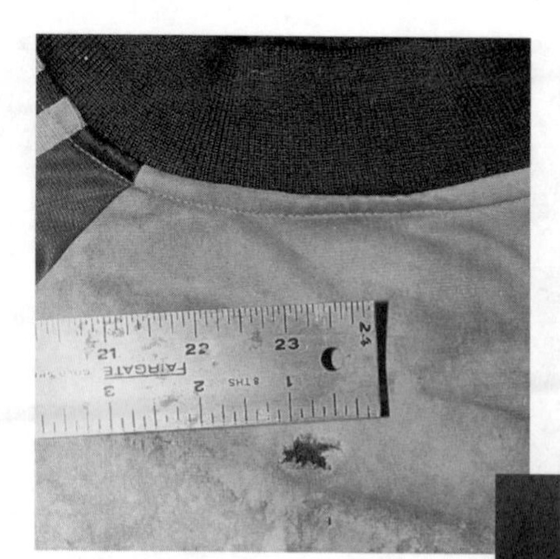

Bullet hole in Walter's sweatsuit top being measured during his autopsy.

Walter Scott before his death in 1983.

Long-time acquaintance of Jim Williams and former St. Charles County Sheriff, Ray Runyon.

Michael Turken, Jim's defense attorney.

Jim Williams incarcerated at the Potosi Correctional Center.

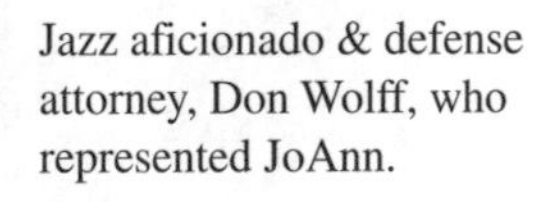

Jazz aficionado & defense attorney, Don Wolff, who represented JoAnn.

Kay and Walter, Sr., as a devoted couple to each other and their son's memory.

Mike Krenski in 1996, the band member who wrote the song 'The Cheater'.

December 25, 1983. Every Christmas morning for three years, Bill and Pat Brown, next door neighbors to the Notheises, would invite everyone in the immediate neighborhood over for a brunch. Even before they had moved into their new home on Pershing Lake Drive, they had become good friends with the Notheis family. Walter, JoAnn, Mindy, and Bryan referred to Bill as "Grandpa." And as soon as Walter came off the road for a few days or a few weeks, he would head next door to visit his neighbors.

The day before Walter and JoAnn had celebrated their fourteenth wedding anniversary. When they entered the Browns' family room for the Christmas morning brunch, it was as if they had just arrived for divorce court. The tension between the two vibrated uneasiness to everyone near them.

The Browns were aware that ever since Walter decided to include two female dancers as part of his act that marital problems between JoAnn and Walter had escalated. JoAnn told Bill and Pat that she wanted him to get rid of them, especially Serina.

Walter refused. They also were cognizant about their neighbor's financial difficulties, owing the IRS back taxes and making hefty payments on numerous loans.

To add to these problems, all the neighbors knew JoAnn was having an affair with Jim and that she wanted out of her marriage so she could marry him. Even the twins knew. But no one believed Walter was aware of it. Until today.

While the neighbors chatted and laughed, Walter kept pacing back and forth in front of the windows, which overlooked the frozen lake behind the house. His face was taut. His eyes wary.

Bill walked over to him and placed a hand on Walter's shoulder. "Hey, settle down. Lookin' for a monster to break through that ice?"

"I'm fine, Bill. Just a bit antsy."

"What you need, fella, is some of this good food," said Bill, pointing to a table in the corner which was covered with egg casseroles, cheese blitzes, Belgian waffles, ham, sausage and bacon, and a multitude of rolls, cakes, and cookies.

Walter shook his head. "Thanks, but I'm not hungry." He peered at JoAnn, who was across the room talking to Bill's daughter-in-law, Claudia.

A few minutes later, Claudia loudly announced, "I'll be right back. I completely forgot the folding table and chairs at home. Walter, JoAnn's going with me to help load them in my car, okay?"

"Why ask me? She normally does what she wants to do without my permission."

All eyes glanced at Walter. All eyes held the secret. Everyone either stopped talking in mid-sentence or continued in hushed whispers until the two women left. Then quickly, the talking resumed. But it was subdued, not as vociferous as before.

▪ ▪ ▪

Claudia lived only a few blocks from her in-laws. Opening the front door, Claudia stood aside and let JoAnn go in first. Jim stood in the foyer with his arms wide open. "Merry Christmas, babe," he said as he grabbed JoAnn, hugging her tightly.

For fifteen minutes Claudia left them alone while she collected the table and chairs to take back to the party.

▪ ▪ ▪

About the same time as his father celebrated a brief Christmas with JoAnn, Jimi Williams, now twenty-three years old and six foot eight, stepped off the bus and hugged his Grandma Almaroad. He had just gotten out of prison again. Throughout the last several years he had been arrested on several felony charges and incarcerated in correctional facilities across the country.

Jimi had always been exceptionally close to his mother. Sharon kept telling everyone that her older son was really a good boy but he just needed some straightening out. When he was jailed, she would write him everyday. When she died, his world folded up for a while. She had been the only person in his life who had loved him unconditionally. With his mother dead only two months, his grandmother said he could live with her.

Before Jimi got out of prison, he talked to his father. Later, in a police statement, Jimi said his father had offered him five hundred dollars to rough someone up during the Christmas holidays. Although Jimi had dealt drugs, ran with an outlaw biker group, stole personal property, and assaulted numerous people, he later emphasized to the police that he was not a murderer.

▪ ▪ ▪

At four o'clock in the afternoon, Walter and his family arrived at his parents to celebrate Christmas. Normally, Walter always entered someone's home by the back door. Today was no exception. After placing his handgun on top of the refrigerator, he gave his mother a big hug.

Apparently the tension between Walter and JoAnn continued from earlier in the day. Now it was JoAnn whose face strained with resentment. While everyone else talked and laughed, she sat sullenly in a corner chair, tapping her fingernails on the wooden armrest. Occasionally, Walter would glance at her, their eyes transmitting discord and contempt. When Kay announced it was time to eat, it was now JoAnn who said she wasn't hungry.

After dinner, they all went into the living room to exchange gifts. The adults gathered around, watching Mindy and Bryan open their gifts first. Amid the scattered red, white, and green paper and ribbon, Kay handed JoAnn and Walter their gifts. The last gift Walter opened from his parents revealed a MacGregor blue and white jogging suit.

"This is great! How did you know I needed a new one? You can bet I'll get a lot of use out of this. Thanks, Mom, Dad."

A short time later, JoAnn wanted to go, but Walter said he wouldn't leave until he saw his brother.

Around ten o'clock Ronnie and his family showed up. More gifts were exchanged. Like his parents, Ronnie also noticed the tension between his brother and JoAnn. Leaning over to Walter, he asked, "What's up?"

"Shit, we had a big fight earlier on. Things aren't going well between us."

JoAnn looked at her watch, then told Walter, "It's getting late and we have another party to go to."

Walter's eyes bored into her. Slowly and precisely, in a low voice he firmly stated, "If I were you, I wouldn't be in a big hurry to go to that party."

She immediately turned her head to look at a picture on the wall next to her, and for the next hour sat silently.

At midnight Walter got on his overcoat to warm up the car for the long ride back to St. Charles. Snow covered the ground and the frigid temperatures dipped below zero. Although JoAnn said she had experienced problems with the battery prior to

Walter flying home, the Lincoln's engine turned over right away.

After loading the trunk with Christmas presents, Walter kissed his parents goodbye. It would be the last time Kay and Walter would see their son.

December 27–28, 1983. The animosity between Walter and JoAnn had not abated. In the early afternoon on December 27, Walter called his mother. After some small talk about the license bureau moving its location, he told Kay he was seriously thinking of selling the house.

"I thought you loved that house, Wally."

"I do, but things aren't going well with JoAnn and me. And everytime I come home, I can't relax much because I have to catch up on things that need to get done around here."

"You'll also have that with any other house you buy."

"I know. That's why I think I might get a condo."

"Would you be happy in one?"

"I'm not sure, Mother. I do love this house." He hesitated for a moment, then asked, "How about you and Dad buying it? Then I'd always have a place to come home to when I'm off the road."

"Wally, we have a home already. Plus, you know I don't want to move all the way out to St. Charles."

"Oh, well, just a thought."

After talking about other things for a short time, they hung up.

■ ■ ■

The day before, Bruce Schone, the owner of Schone's Automotive, called Walter and told him he would be in the garage all the next day. Walter needed to get a state inspection sticker for the Lincoln. Schone didn't do the actual state inspection, but he could get it through another garage owner who would write one up for him when he requested it. Earlier, he had told Walter to drop by the paperwork. At four o'clock Walter drove up to Schone's to also check on a battery for the car, since JoAnn continued to complain about having had trouble starting the Lincoln.

As soon as Walter left, JoAnn placed a call to Jim's mobile phone. Because heavy snow was once more predicted for later that night, Jim had gone to Hackmann Lumber on Highway 94 South to buy a snow shovel.

"He just left," she told Jim.

"Where?"

"To Bruce's. He's supposed to see about an inspection sticker and check on a battery for the car."

"Thanks, babe. Think I'll take a little ride over to Ken's Auto Supply."

Ken's Auto Supply was directly across from Bruce Schone's place. Jim stayed by the front window of the store, glancing at cans of oil, air filters and other merchandise on the counters, while mainly staring toward the garage. After half an hour, he saw Walter start for his Lincoln. Jim quickly walked out the front door, sat in his truck, and watched Walter pull out. He followed his lover's husband for a few minutes, then veered down another road.

Every Tuesday at six-thirty, Jim bowled at Harvest Lanes on a team he sponsored. Being an avid bowler, he never missed a night. Tonight, he would later tell the police, he simply forgot all about it. Instead, he said he ordered a pizza to go from Pizza Hut, stopped by a convenience store for soda and cigarettes, then went home for the rest of the evening.

■ ■ ■

During dinner the television blared while the Notheis family ate. A television reporter for the local news mentioned a follow-up on the body of a St. Louis businessman which police found in the trunk of a car at the airport. It was alleged to be a "mob hit."

Walter looked at his family and said, "When I die, I want a big party where everyone's laughing and having a good time. No tears. No sadness."

At first Bryan wondered why his father said this, but he soon dismissed the remark and continued eating.

After dinner, Walter and the twins went into the family room to watch a movie on television. Around seven o'clock the phone rang. JoAnn came into the room.

"Walter, it's Bruce."

Instead of using the phone next to him on the end table, he walked into the kitchen to talk. A few minutes later, he returned to the couch and continued watching the movie with his children.

Several minutes passed. JoAnn stood at the doorway. "Aren't you going?"

"There's no hurry."

"He might close soon. I think you should go."

Walter looked at her, reached for his deck shoes near the coffee table, and slowly put them on. He had on the blue and white jogging suit his parents had given him for Christmas. Taking his brown and gold CPO jacket out of the hall closet, he poked his head back into the room and said, "See you in a little bit, kids. Need to head up to Bruce's." He left by the kitchen door to the garage.

A few minutes later, JoAnn came into the room and told her two children, "I'm going to one of the neighbor's who's having a party. See you later." She left by the front door.

■ ■ ■

As Walter left his house on Pershing Lake Drive, Jimi Williams began his new job at Hurley's Show Bar in Marion, Illinois. At six o'clock his grandmother drove her grandson to Hurley's. Alice Almaroad also went into the bar and spoke with Mr. Hurley at one end of the bar, while other personnnel showed Jimi the pool tables, explained about the cover charge and other details regarding the club. Within half an hour, Jimi's grandmother drove back home. Around two o'clock in the morning of December 28, 1983, she returned to the club to take her grandson home.

After that night, Jimi found his own means to the club. His grandmother later testified in court about that night and how Jimi could hitchhike anywhere without much of a problem.

■ ■ ■

Bruce Schone knew Walter, Jim, and JoAnn. He also was well acquainted with both of Jim's sons, especially Jimi. Not only did Schone own the automotive garage, but from June, 1981, until April, 1982, he also owned a bar in St. Charles. The bar catered to a rough clientele, some using it as a contact place to make drug deals. Police officials stated that Schone also had dealt drugs. It was in this bar that someone had shot Jimi in his side over a drug deal.

■ ■ ■

The night of December 27 was bitterly cold and several inches of snow had already fallen. Around nine o'clock Schone called

Walter's house. Joann answered.

"Hey, where's Walter?" Schone asked.

"What do you mean? Hasn't he shown up yet?"

"Nope, but you know how Walter is. He tells me he's bringing his car in at a certain time and may not show up for a day or two."

Walter had a notorious reputation of never being where he would say he would be going. If he went to the quick shop for a pack of cigarettes, he might have stopped by a friend's house to visit for three or four hours. His parents, his first wife, his second wife, and most people close to him, all knew that Walter's whereabouts were unpredictable, except when he was performing. He also never called to let someone know where he was. Eventually, he would show up, whether at ten in the evening, or five or six the next morning.

Schone continued, "I'll wait around for about ten more minutes, then I'm closing up and going home."

▪ ▪ ▪

During the investigation, the police received several different versions of what occurred the evening after Walter left his house. JoAnn stated that she returned home from the party around eight-thirty. At nine o'clock, she said it was she who called the garage, and that Schone told her Walter had never arrived. At nine-thirty, Schone called to tell her he was closing up. She told the police she then watched television and fell asleep until three o'clock in the morning, at which time she became concerned and called the Sheriff's department to inquire about auto accidents. At six-thirty she again called the police to make a missing person's report.

▪ ▪ ▪

When JoAnn had made the police statement, she failed to tell them that around one-thirty or two in the morning on December

28, 1983, she had called Scott and Chris Henderson, long-time friends of hers and Walter's. Scott had been a police officer with the Jennings Police Department, and at one time he and his wife had been neighbors of the Notheises in St. Louis. He later testified that JoAnn called to ask how to file a missing person's report on Walter.

"I'm really concerned, Scott. Walter said he was going up to this garage to get an inspection sticker and a battery. But he never got there."

"You called the garage, right?" asked Scott.

"Yeah, around nine or so."

"Do you think he went somewhere else, like to a party? You know how Walter takes off, saying he's heading someplace but goes the opposite direction."

"I don't think so. He was only wearing a sweatsuit. And you know how picky Walter is about his image if he's going out to where a lot of people will be." She also told him that Walter only had a couple of credit cards and his driver's license with him.

"It's doubtful anything's happened, but to alleviate your anxiety, why don't you call the Sheriff's department in St. Charles and see if he's possibly been involved in an accident. If they don't have anything, call the Highway Patrol about accident reports. And if nothing there, call the emergency rooms of the hospitals in St. Charles."

"Okay, but what if they don't know anything?" asked JoAnn.

"You're sure there was no party or anyplace else where he could have gone?"

JoAnn hesitated, then stated, "Well, I know he went downtown to the Mansion House Center." The Mansion House Center had recently been in the news regarding several mob-related bombings.

"Did he tell you that?"

"Uh, no. I contacted a friend of mine, Jim Williams, on his mobile phone as Walter was getting ready to leave. Later, Jim called me and said he had followed Walter down to the Mansion

House Center and saw him pull into the parking area. Then Jim came back to St. Charles."

For the next two hours until four o'clock in the morning, Scott and Chris Henderson passed the phone back and forth across the bed as they talked to JoAnn.

▪ ▪ ▪

Jim Williams' account of the night Walter disappeared was that JoAnn had called him at nine o'clock and again at at nine-thirty. She told Jim she was worried because Walter had never shown up at Schone's garage. She even said she tried calling Schone's wife, who also worked at Fairmount Elementary, but no one answered. JoAnn added that Walter wasn't dressed appropriately to be out on such a wintry night. She then decided she would wait awhile before contacting the police.

At ten-fifteen, Jim said she called again.

"I'm really worried. It's snowing so hard. There must be four or five inches of snow on the ground already. I think I might call the State Patrol and some hospitals to see if he's been in an accident."

"Okay. Well, keep me posted. If he doesn't show up, call me in the morning."

Jim stated that it was around four or five in the morning on December 28, 1983, that JoAnn called him again.

"He's still not home."

"Let me call a friend of mine who's a deputy. I'll see what he has to say."

When Jim talked to Ray Runyon, who later became the Sheriff of St. Charles County, he told Jim that normally a missing person's report for an adult isn't made out for twenty-four hours. But if JoAnn would feel better about it, she could call and file one in the morning.

The police report stated JoAnn had called the Sheriff's department at three o'clock. Because such a short period of time had passed, the officer told her to call back later in the day. Around seven o'clock she called once more and insisted that a report be made.

▪ ▪ ▪

When Sheriff Ray Runyon later testified in court about the incident, he recalled that Jim had contacted him between one and two o'clock in the morning on December 28, 1983, and told him he was calling from JoAnn's house. Because Jim had been the county electrical inspector for three years, and later a well known and influential businessman in St. Charles County, numerous people knew and liked him. Runyon had not only known Jim for more than fifteen years, but he had known Sharon and the two boys, especially Jimi and his trouble with the law. Besides knowing Jim's family, Runyon also knew that Jim had been carrying on an affair with JoAnn for a year, using Schone's garage as an occasional meeting place to leave one of the cars. And he knew that Jim was obsessively in love with JoAnn Notheis.

"Why are you calling from JoAnn's?"

"The lady is concerned about her husband missing and her son, Bryan, is also worried."

"How long have you been there?"

"Most of the night."

"How long has he been gone?"

"Six, seven hours."

"You know how Scott is. He's probably with some woman."

"Naw. JoAnn said he wasn't dressed to impress. He only had on a jogging suit."

"It's still too soon. Tell her to wait until the morning at least. And, Jim, it's not wise for you to be there. Suppose he shows up? I hear he has a hot temper and carries a gun."

"Hey, I'll face that bridge if I have to. I'm not afraid of the man."

"Be careful. And let me know what's happening."

▪ ▪ ▪

At three o'clock in the morning on December 28, 1983, Kay Notheis woke up out of a sound sleep. Her whole body was chilled, as if she were enfolded in a blanket of ice. She had a gnawing feeling that something was wrong. Moving closer to her husband for warmth, she eventually went back to sleep.

Close to seven o'clock, the phone rang.

"Hi, Mom. It's JoAnn. Is Walter there?"

"No, he's not. Why?"

"He never came home last night and I'm really worried.

"Were you two arguing?"

"No. He left at seven to go to Schone's garage to get an inspection sticker and a new battery for the car. I called the garage around nine, but he hadn't shown up."

"You know how Walter is. Maybe he went to a party and stayed the night at someone's house."

"He wasn't dressed for a party. He was wearing the jogging suit you gave him for Christmas, deck shoes, and his brown and yellow CPO jacket. I just have this gut feeling that something's happened to him."

"Did you call the police?"

"Yeah, I just called the sheriff's office and they're sending someone over pretty soon to make out a missing person's report."

"Do you want us to come over?"

"Yes, that would be a good idea."

Kay urged her husband to get dressed so they could drive over to St. Charles. But Walter, Sr., wasn't concerned since he knew his son frequently stayed out all night, not returning home until sometime the next morning.

Kay continued to feel a hollowness in the pit of her stomach. She nagged and prodded her husband until they finally pulled out of their driveway around ten o'clock.

▪ ▪ ▪

When Kay and Walter arrived at Walter and JoAnn's house, it was close to eleven. Mindy let them in the front door and told her grandparents that her mom was in the breakfast room. As Kay and Walter walked into the kitchen, they saw their daughter-in-law sitting next to a large dark-haired man. Their son's briefcase was opened and this man held up one of Walter's rings toward the overhead light as he examined it with a magnifying glass.

He said, "This ring is good." Then picking up other pieces, he continued, "This one's junk, but here's another good piece."

JoAnn looked up to see her in-laws standing at the doorway and solemnly stated, "Mom, Dad, this is a friend of mine, Jim Williams. He did the electrical work on the downstairs apartment."

Kay and Walter just looked at him and nodded.

Also laying on the table were a pocket watch, a gold toothpick, and two handguns.

Walter pointed to the guns. "Are those Wally's?"

Jim nodded. "They sure are. I took the bullets out."

"Why did you do that?"

Jim pointed to Bryan who was standing next to JoAnn. "Because I didn't want the kids to get hurt."

"So, what have you heard?" Kay asked JoAnn.

"Nothing. The police came by around seven-thirty and I made a missing person's report."

"No one's heard from him?"

"No, that's why I called his guitarist, Ed Eckert, and told him I thought we should begin canceling some of Walter's engagements."

Kay's eyes opened wide. "Isn't this too soon?"

"He'd be back now if he was okay," replied JoAnn.

After glancing at her husband, Kay continued to question JoAnn. "What did Ed say?"

"He said to wait. That Walter is too professional to miss a performance. But I told him we should do it right away."

Kay stared at her daughter-in-law. "But you're canceling some bookings that are more than seven weeks off. Why?"

"Well, I have a feeling he's not coming back to do these, and I don't want to be the one who has to pay the late penalty fee if I don't cancel within a certain time.

▪ ▪ ▪

Later that day, JoAnn called Bob Curtis, Walter's business manager in New Jersey, and told him to cancel Walter's New Year's Eve show at the Poconos in Pennsylvania and other engagements he had booked elsewhere. Curtis urged her to hold off, especially since the Poconos show would be Walter's highest paid performance for one night: four thousand dollars. But JoAnn ignored his advice. She also called the Playboy Club and the Hoffman House in St. Louis to cancel the next nine weeks. Walter had been missing less than twenty-four hours.

▪ ▪ ▪

Early the same afternoon JoAnn called Linn Wise, a friend and neighbor, who was at another neighbor's house, Bill Callabrese's. "Linn, I want to know if you've seen or heard from Walter since seven o'clock last night?"

"Sure haven't. Why what's up?"

"He left to go to Bruce Schone's garage after dinner. He never showed up there, and never came back home."

"Gee, JoAnn, I don't know what to tell you. Anything we can do to help?"

"Could you sort of look for his car at shopping malls, you know, Chesterfield and Northwest Plaza? And, uh, maybe when you're over at Northwest, check out the airport. Bryan just remembered that a few weeks ago some guy's body was found in the trunk of his car at the airport. Last night the news said it was mob-related. And you know how Walter associates with a lot of shady characters."

"Sure. Bill and I'll head out right away."

After driving around several shopping centers, scouring the parking lots for Walter's car, both men drove to Lambert Field. They slowly went up one row and down another in the short-term parking garage. Nothing. Agreeing it was not there, they headed to the top level to exit. Linn tapped Bill on his shoulder. "Take a look at that," he said, pointing to a 1978 dark green Lincoln Town car with a white vinyl top.

Bill asked, "Do you think that's Walter's?"

"I'm not sure, but it sure looks like it."

They both got out of their car and brushed a thin layer of snow away from a side window. Peering inside, they didn't see anything suspicious. After jotting down the license plate number, they returned to St. Charles and called JoAnn. She verified it was Walter's car.

A short time later she called them again. "Linn, would you and Bill go back to the airport and bring the car back here?"

"Sure. No problem."

"Good. Jim said he'll take both of you over. He should be by in a few minutes."

As Jim drove them over in his pickup truck, both Linn and Bill began growing apprehensive.

Bill said, "I hope we don't find anything."

Linn added, "Yeah, suppose we pop open the trunk and there's Walter's body?"

Jim turned to his two passengers. "Don't worry. There's nothing there. He's long gone. I doubt you'll ever see him again."

Both men quickly looked at each other, each silently acknowledging a gut-wrenching fear that their driver knew what had happened to Walter.

▪ ▪ ▪

Meanwhile, when Scott Henderson and his wife, Chris, came home around four-thirty that same afternoon, they decided to drive around the airport to see if Walter's car could possibly be there. Later, as they were interviewed by Detectives Blankenship and Kaiser, Scott Henderson told the police officers that when he and his wife pulled to the upper level, which is an open-air parking area, they spotted the car. Four or five inches of snow covered the top of it, but there was no snow under the car, indicating it had been at the airport for some time.

After notifying the airport police that they had found Walter's automobile, they drove over to JoAnn's. She informed them that some other people had found the car earlier and were in the process of bringing it back.

▪ ▪ ▪

When Jim, Linn, and Bill arrived at Lambert Field, the St. Louis airport police refused to allow them to take the car. After Jim called JoAnn telling her of the problem, Scott Henderson, being a former police officer, called Lt. Crandle of the airport police to see if Walter's brother, Ron, could sign the release form. They consented.

The airport authorities said that Walter's car was logged in at the lot on December 27 between ten o'clock and midnight. Betty Klaus, an employee of the airport garage, told Detectives Wacker and Shoemake, "Each night after midnight the parking areas are checked and license plates are recorded on a log as to their location. The Lincoln's license number, ZLH-343, was logged on the blue level at midnight."

Once Ron arrived at the office of the airport police, Patrolman DeVaney directed him to Walter's car. As Ron and his wife got out of their car and walked up to the three men standing by the Lincoln, they saw that the car had already been opened and searched.

Jim told him, "These airport police are letting their ass get in the way of their mouth. They won't let us take the car back, even though JoAnn authorized it over the phone."

Ron's temper flared. He ignored Jim and turned to DeVaney. "Who in the hell gave anyone permission to enter Walter's car? You had to wait until I got here."

DeVaney took Ron aside and tried to explain the situation. He told Ron he had personally examined Walter's vehicle and found no signs of foul play nor any type of stains. JoAnn also told DeVaney that it was all right for these men to bring the car back to her residence. Ron pointed over to Jim, who was talking with Linn and Bill. "See that big guy there? I know he's done something to my brother."

At the time the airport police released the car to Ron, it had not been processed. Despite the airport police giving it a cursory exam, no fingerprints were ever taken.

After Ron signed the release form, he and his wife drove over to Walter and JoAnn's house. Jim gave Walter's car keys to Linn and Bill, and everyone headed back to St. Charles.

▪ ▪ ▪

By this time, most of the neighbors and numerous friends congregated at JoAnn's. When they walked into the house, JoAnn greeted them with hugs and tears. Twenty-four hours earlier Walter had been watching a movie with his children in the very room which was now filled with people either standing or sitting. Some speculated about where he could be; others spoke about their New Year's Eve plans.

Early in the evening JoAnn walked up to her in-laws and said, "Tomorrow I think I'll fly to Harrisburg and get the Suburban and trailer. I need to call Ed Eckert later to see if he can drive it back. Could you both stay with the twins tomorrow and tomorrow night?"

Kay said, "We'll be here. Let us know what time."

Then Jim looked at JoAnn and said, "You know, I can use the trailer in my business."

Kay beaded her eyes into this stranger in her son's house. "Let's not bury him 'til we find him."

That night Jim spent the night at JoAnn's. Everyone knew about Walter's propensity for jealousy. Everyone knew he carried a gun. Yet Jim said that Bryan was afraid and asked him to spend the night. To appease the eleven year old, he slept on his lover's couch.

December 29–30, 1983. The previous evening, JoAnn had called Walter's guitarist and road manager, Ed Eckert, telling him that all scheduled performances had been canceled in cities on the east coast and St. Louis. She then asked him if he and David Kanter, Walter's drummer, would drive the Suburban and trailer back from Pennsylvania to St. Louis. She also called Frank Floto in Mechanicsburg, Pennsylvania, and asked if he would pick her up at the airport the next evening.

Lastly, she called Serina. JoAnn told her not to go to Poconos for the New Year's Eve show because of Walter's disappearance. A short time later when the police interviewed Walter's dancer and lover, she added that during the conversation JoAnn did not express concern about her husband's whereabouts.

Walter's parents arrived back at JoAnn's in the morning on December 29. Earlier, Kay had told her husband that perhaps he should accompany JoAnn to Harrisburg. He refused. He said, "If she wanted me to go with her, she would have asked."

When they walked in the front door, again they saw Jim Williams. After half an hour, Jim and JoAnn left, JoAnn wearing the blue fox fur coat that Walter had given her for Christmas. Since Jim could fly free for one year after Sharon's death, and JoAnn indicated she didn't have any money, he insisted on paying for her air fare. Kay had assumed Jim was just driving JoAnn to the airport, but shortly after they left, Mindy told her grandparents, "No, Mr. Williams is going up to Pennsylvania with Mom." That's when Walter's parents became suspicious of Jim and JoAnn.

▪ ▪ ▪

Frank Floto owned two music stores called the Juke Box, which specialized in the late '50's to mid-'60's Motown songs. After attending many of Walter's performances in Pennsylvania, they became friends. Eventually, he told Walter that he could store his truck and trailer at his house when Walter would head home to St. Louis.

When Floto picked JoAnn up at the airport, he was surprised to see a big man with her. From the way Jim asked questions, Floto initially thought Jim was a police detective. He later stated to the police that neither JoAnn nor Jim seemed concerned with finding Walter. Instead, they kept asking Floto if he knew about any bank accounts or "stashed" cash that Walter had. Floto knew nothing.

Upon reaching his house, Floto gave them a flashlight. Jim and JoAnn first searched the truck. Finding nothing, they walked back to the trailer. Only Floto and Walter had keys to it, that was why he was surprised to see Jim take a set out of his pants pocket and open up the trailer. In a police report, Floto stated that JoAnn directed Jim on which suitcases to leave alone, since the only personal belongings she seemed interested in were those of Walter's and Serina's.

"This one looks like a woman's, but it's locked."

"Break it open," JoAnn demanded. "I know there's money in here somewhere, or at least some information about bank accounts. Maybe he had Serina hide it with her things."

As they began going through Serina's clothing and makeup, JoAnn turned to Floto and said, "Ed and Dave should be landing shortly. We need to continue searching through this stuff. Could you pick them up, Frank?"

"Sure. No problem."

When Eckert, Kanter, and Floto returned from the airport, JoAnn and Jim were in the house sitting on the couch. Her face was contorted in rage. Pointing to a box on the table, she bitterly asked Walter's two musicians, "What do you know about this?"

Eckert and Kanter looked inside. They saw a variety of pornographic magazines, sexual devices, and Polaroid pictures of Walter and Serina engaged in a multitude of sexual positions, using several sex toys, including a penis extension. Later, information from a police statement indicated that Walter and Serina had belonged to a couple of "swinger" clubs. There were other people in some of the pictures.

A few days later when Captain Tom Bishop conducted a telephone interview with Serina, he asked, "Who took the pictures?"

She embarrassingly replied, "My mother."

Both Eckert and Kanter were surprised. Walter had always insisted that no band member was to do any drugs, be a chronic drinker, nor fraternize with the dancers. If anyone committed one of these infractions, Walter said they would be gone.

"JoAnn, honest. I don't know anything about this at all," stated Eckert.

"That son-of-a-bitch! I knew he was having an affair with Serina, but he kept lying to me, denying it everytime I asked him about it. That bastard! I told him three years ago to get rid of the bitch, that she'd just cause a lot of shit between us, but he kept her on anyway."

Eckert and Kanter didn't know what to say, and looked down

at the floor.

Jim grabbed JoAnn's hand and patted it. She then took a deep breath and asked, "Do either of you know about money that Walter may have hidden somewhere, like bank accounts in Pennsylvania, Atlantic City?"

Both shook their heads no.

"How about some jewelry?"

Again, both had no knowledge of this either.

"Somehow with what he made, he should have been sending a lot more home than he did. I only got five hundred a week and I know he brought in at least twenty-five hundred."

"JoAnn, I only know that after Walter paid the band members, he had around eight hundred left. Three hundred he kept for his expenses and five hundred he sent to you," Eckert said.

After talking quietly to Jim for a few minutes, she turned to the two band members again. "Are you driving back tonight?"

"Yeah, we thought we would."

Jim got up and took two one-hundred bills from his gold money clip. "Here's some cash. In case you need it."

Eckert said, "No, that's all right."

"No, I insist. It'll pay for the gas, some food, and your time to do this."

Finally Eckert relented. "Well, okay. Thanks a lot."

JoAnn then phoned the St. Charles County Sheriff's office to tell them she had made arrangements to bring Walter's Suburban and trailer back. But no one called any Pennsylvania law enforcement office to dust for fingerprints or check for possible clues.

Before Eckert and Kanter left, JoAnn told them, "You can stop in Greenville to drop off the suitcases and equipment to some of the band members there."

Eckert asked, "Should I stop in Indiana and give Serina her stuff?"

"Absolutely not!" Jim commanded. "Drive straight through

Indiana without any stops at all. Understand?"

JoAnn added, "If she wants her things, she'll have to come to St. Louis and meet with me personally to get them."

"All right. If that's what you want."

The entire time the two band members talked with Jim and JoAnn at Floto's house, neither of them were questioned nor heard any mention about Walter's possible whereabouts. JoAnn's biggest concern, they said, was finding money or jewelry. And once she found the photographs, she told Floto, "It's a good thing he's gone because I was going to leave him anyway after the first of the year. In fact, for the past two and a half years I've been wanting a divorce."

While Eckert and Kanter began getting the Suburban and trailer ready for the trip back to St. Louis, JoAnn asked Floto to take her and Jim to the Holiday Inn close to the airport. Despite Jim having sufficient money on him for two rooms, they registered for only one. He later told people it was cheaper, and that after such a tumultuous two days, neither of them wanted to be alone.

▪ ▪ ▪

Part way through Indiana, Eckert looked in his rearview mirror and saw flashing lights. "Aw, shit, what's going on now?"

Apparently, someone had called Serina and informed her that JoAnn had flown up to Floto's place, broken into the luggage, and found the explicit pictures. She called the Indiana State Police and had Eckert stopped. The police told them to proceed to Terra Haute, where Serina was staying with her sister.

Upon arriving there, Serina drove up to meet them. Her face emitted deep concern. "I know something's happened to Walter. He would have called me if he were in trouble or if he left JoAnn because of a fight. Did she say anything to you two?"

"No. Just be careful. She's pretty upset about finding those pictures of you and Walter."

Serina looked chagrined and averted her eyes downward for a few seconds. Collecting her composure, she said, "This is like a nightmare. I can't believe any of this is happening. And I'm so worried about Walter. When was the last time you heard from him?"

Eckert replied, "A couple of days after we got back to St. Louis. He came over to pick up his clothes that I brought back for him. Otherwise, nothing."

"If you hear anything, give me a call. Promise?"

"Sure will."

Serina made all of the costumes for herself and the other dancer. Because she put a lot of time and money into constructing them, she knew that once JoAnn had them in her possession, she would never see them again. Grabbing all of her luggage, containing her personal items and her outfits, Serina thanked the two band members and returned to her sister's.

▪ ▪ ▪

Early in the morning on December 30, 1983, as Kay and Walter sat in the breakfast room talking, they both thought it was odd that the day following Walter's disappearance there was a throng of neighbors in every corner of the house. But in the twenty-four hours they had been at their son's house with the twins, only one neighbor, "Doc" Spraul, stopped by to check on any new developments regarding Walter.

Later that same morning as they lingered over a late breakfast with the twins, JoAnn stormed through the door and flung a bag onto the kitchen counter. Her voice filled with rage. "This is what your wonderful son has been doing. Go on. Take a look at this."

"No, JoAnn, I don't think I will," replied Kay.

Jim, who had followed JoAnn into the kitchen, leaned against one of the cabinets. He looked down at Walter's parents, placed his hands on Bryan's shoulders, and said, "You have no idea what your son has done to this family."

Kay looked up at this stranger in her son's house and responded, "How do you know?"

JoAnn took off the blue fox coat and threw it to Mindy. "Take this upstairs and get the receipt off of my dresser. I'm taking this son-of-a-bitch back."

Kay and Walter quickly gathered their things, told JoAnn to call them if she heard anything about their son, and left.

That evening Jim and JoAnn invited Scott and Chris Henderson over to Jim's house for dinner. Within a short period of time, the Henderson's, who had been good friends of Walter's for years, soon socialized with Jim and JoAnn.

▪ ▪ ▪

The next morning JoAnn called Kay. Immediately, Kay asked, "Have you heard anything about Wally?"

Kay still detected a lot of anger in JoAnn's voice, "No, and that's not why I called. I found a cashier's check receipt for over four thousand dollars made out to Dad. I want to know what that was for."

"Walter's not here right now. When he returns, I'll have him call you back."

An hour later Walter called his daughter-in-law. "JoAnn, that was for partial payment on a debt for some money I loaned Wally."

JoAnn's irritation increased. She responded, "I want you to know that the money to pay for your retirement party came out of my household money."

"Well, I don't know anything about that."

With a loud breath of exasperation, JoAnn said, "I can't talk anymore. Goodbye."

▪ ▪ ▪

Later in the day, Kay tried calling JoAnn. After three rings, the operator answered, "That number has been changed."

Kay was bewildered. She then asked, "What's the new number?"

"It's unlisted and I can't give it out."

"It's my son's house, his number. He's disappeared and I need to find out if my daughter-in-law has heard anything since this morning."

"I'm sorry, ma'm, but I'm not allowed to reveal the new number, no matter what the circumstances are."

Kay hung up. She looked at her husband, blinked her eyes and said, "I know they've done something to Wally. She just got an unlisted number. Now we can't reach her unless we go over to the house."

From that morning, neither of them ever spoke to JoAnn again.

January–August, 1984. Upon returning to St. Louis after searching Walter's trailer, JoAnn's anger mounted. Concern and grief, which would be a normal reaction for a wife whose husband had just disappeared, was not evident. From all indications, their marriage had wallowed in estrangement for several years. Jealousy, obstinacy, and difficulty to trust others were traits both JoAnn and Walter possessed, ultimately contributing to the dissipation of their passionate love. With the affair between her husband and Serina confirmed, JoAnn probably felt psychologically raped. Walter had violated her hard-earned trust. And despite her affair with Jim, people who knew her said she had never loved any man as she had Walter. That was why her hate erupted into intense fury.

On January 1, 1984, JoAnn called Serina Michaels. When Serina answered, JoAnn immediately said, "I know all about you and Walter."

"What do you mean?" asked Serina.

"You little bitch, you know what I mean. I have the pictures of you and Walter fucking. And I have all your sexual gadgets. Plus the letters you wrote him. You calling him "Bear" and "Boo." I told him to get rid of you right after he hired you. That you'd be nothing but trouble. What do you have to say about this?"

"Nothing," Serina quietly replied.

"Well, I sure don't need Walter around to get a divorce. He's not getting a dime. Everything's already in my name. So, if you want Walter because you think he has a lot of money, you're a bigger damn fool than I thought."

Serina's embarrassment added to her being easily intimidated by JoAnn. She was only twenty-three; JoAnn, thirty-eight. Although the sexual relationship between her and Walter was consensual, as well as the sexual acts of being photographed, she was nevertheless naive and vulnerable. She loved Walter, and now Walter's wife knew about them.

She had nothing more to say.

▪ ▪ ▪

Normally when a person is reported missing, a couple of detectives handle the routine investigation. Once Walter did not turn up in the Poconos for his New Year's Eve show, the police felt they were onto something big. After discovering that JoAnn and Jim were lovers, and that Jim's wife had died from a minor automobile accident two months earlier, suspicions grew. But it wasn't until the police found out that Jim had spent the night at Walter and JoAnn's house on December 28, and that he had accompanied her to Harrisburg, searched the trailer, and stayed together in the same motel room that the Major Case Squad of Greater St. Louis got involved.

Two co-commanders headed this investigation team: Captain Daniel Chapman of the Dellwood Police Department and Captain Robert Wes Simcox of the St. Charles County Sheriff's Department. The report officer was Detective Dennis Cordia of the Florissant Police Department. Eleven other detectives throughout the metropolitan St. Louis area were assigned to cover this intense probe in trying to find Walter Scott. From the St. Charles County Sheriff's Department they were Captain Tom Bishop, Lt. Ken Brockel, Sgt. David Kaiser, Sgt. Donald Messner, Detectives Bernard Duraski, Walter Blankenship, and Steve Roach. In St. Louis the officers were Detective Terry Shoemake of the Jennings Police Department, Detective John Rueckert of Bellefontaine Neighbors Police Department, Sgt. Robert Wacker of Bridgeton Police Department, and Detective Donald Bortz of the Ferguson Police Department.

About this time, Officer Copeland, the deputy who suspected something amiss with Sharon Williams' demise in October, voiced his belief that her death did not result from the accident. The detectives also launched an investigation into Sharon's death.

Wes Simcox, already head of the criminal investigations division of the St. Charles County Sheriff's Department, and now acting as co-commander of the Major Case Squad, brought JoAnn and Jim individually into his office for further questioning.

JoAnn had previously given a detailed account of Walter's activities, from the time he flew home on December 19 through the night of his disappearance, to Deputy A. C. Blanks. After she returned from the Poconos, the police picked up the .22 and .25-caliber handguns which had belonged to Walter. JoAnn also gave them a bag of capsules that Bryan said he found in his dad's Suburban. These were later analyzed as being Darvon and Valium.

On January 3, 1984, JoAnn walked into Simcox's office. Although she still fumed with anger from her discovery in Pennsylvania, she did cooperate in answering questions. She admitted that when Walter was home, no one could pinpoint where he would go when he left the house, or when he would return. In her statement she also divulged information that she would like to marry Jim and had discussed it with Mindy and Bryan. Yet when she had approached Walter and told him that she wanted out of the marriage, he adamantly refused to even consider it.

As the conversation gravitated to her husband's affair with Serina, JoAnn placed the box of pornographic magazines and sexual gadgets on top of Wes's desk. Then taking the pornographic pictures out of her purse, she laid them out on the desk also. This was the man she had relentlessly pursued for years because of her overwhelming love for him. This was the man who said he couldn't live without her. This was the father of their two beautiful children. And as she looked down at the explicit sexual poses, she saw this same man making love to another woman.

Suddenly, hate welled in her eyes and filled the room with her wrath. The top half of her body trembled with rage. Simcox said that she looked him straight in his eyes and vehemently uttered, "I don't care what's happened to him!"

On January 4, 1984, Detectives Ken Brockel and Walter Blankenship of the St. Charles County Sheriff's Department interviewed Jim Williams. He gave a detailed account of his activities the evening of December 27, including JoAnn's call to him that Walter had left for Schone's garage at four o'clock. When the detectives asked why he had called JoAnn at seven o'clock the same evening, knowing that Walter might be home, Jim answered that he knew Walter had gone back to Schone's. As they further inquired how he knew this, the detectives said Jim then became evasive.

▪ ▪ ▪

The Major Case Squad sent a team of detectives out to investigate people who knew Walter, from his parents to JoAnn's father to neighbors and friends to members of the band. No one had seen Walter after seven o'clock on December 27, 1983. When the detectives went to Bob Kuban's home, the first thing he asked was, "What army did this?" He said Walter had to know the person or persons who killed him because he would never have allowed himself to get into such a situation. He also told the detectives about the conversation in the fall when JoAnn wanted Kuban and Walter to each take out a one hundred thousand dollar insurance policy on each other.

One of the detectives looked at Kuban and said, "Well, that's it." And he pointed his finger at the bandleader. "They wanted you to have a major insurance policy on him so that you would look like the main suspect."

Detectives Brockel and Kaiser interviewed JoAnn's father, John Calcaterra. He stated he had loaned Walter money for back taxes, house payments, and construction loans. When questioned about JoAnn and Walter's relationship, he told the detectives that they didn't have the best of marriages. They also found out that John Calcaterra and Scott Henderson went to Schone's garage with Walter's Lincoln, picked up the inspection sticker, had the battery replaced, and dropped off registration information to have his 1982 Suburban inspected.

When the detectives interviewed Bruce Schone, they asked why he had been so concerned to stay open until nine-thirty waiting for Walter to show up when it was snowing like hell that night. He clammed up. "I don't know anything. I told the first cop all I know and there's nothin' more to say. If you ask me, I think I'm being set up."

"Okay, Schone, then how about taking a polygraph?"

"No way! I've retained two attorneys, Tom Burke and Joel Eisenstein, and they've advised me not to answer any more questions."

Other detectives interviewed many of Walter's neighbors. No one had seen or heard anything strange the night Walter had disappeared. Most of the neighbors were aware of the affair between JoAnn and Jim, and those who had met him liked the big man. They said he had a good sense of humor, was friendly, and treated JoAnn lovingly. Several people stated that Jim seemed to be completely infatuated with her.

▪ ▪ ▪

During one of JoAnn's interviews, she stated that perhaps Walter's disappearance could have been mob or drug related. Even Ronnie Notheis stated that his brother sometimes hung around with unsavory characters. He stated, "They were the type that come out of the woodwork after dark."

One source said that a mob organization known as "the Company" in New Orleans could have been responsible. At one time Walter had canceled a performance with a club in New Orleans that was supposedly mob-owned. Instead, he played at its competitor's. Walter also had a reputation of being a gambler and he could have been heavily in debt to someone. Then there was Walter's connection with Bruce Schone, who, the police stated, had dealt drugs and had had a felony charge of accepting stolen property.

Despite these accusations, when the police interviewed all of Walter's band members and people who knew him well, no one concurred with the above allegations. Every member of the band stated emphatically that Walter was very strict about drugs, drinking, curfews, and neatness. David Kanter, the drummer, said in the four years he had played with Walter's band, he had never known him to do any drugs whatsoever or excessively drink. He also stated that Walter told new band members he would immediately fire anyone caught doing drugs. They all acknowledged that Walter did like to gamble, but he was like most people who go to a casino. He allowed himself a certain amount of money to take, and if he lost it, he would stop playing.

▪ ▪ ▪

On January 4, 1984, Detective Blankenship received a call from one of the twins, Mindy Notheis. The eleven year old told him that she made an error in a previous report she gave to the police when she said that no one called after Bruce Schone had telephoned her father around seven o'clock on December 27. Now she stated that she remembered that Jim Williams had called right after her father left and he asked for her mother. During her call, Blankenship said he had heard muffled voices in the background and that Mindy seemed very hesitant in her speech.

"Are you being told to call me?"

After a few seconds of silence, Mindy quietly replied, "Yes."

"Did your mother tell you to call me and tell me this?"

Another long pause. "Yes."

▪ ▪ ▪

The next day Alec Cundiff, a St. Charles attorney, received a call from JoAnn, who explained the disappearance of her husband and wanted advice about her responsibilities regarding Walter's debts. She then asked him if she could take a polygraph exam. Cundiff said he thought the police would allow it. He also added that since her case seemed to be of a criminal nature, she should contact another attorney who could assist her, as he handled only civil matters.

Later that day, Sergeant Messner and Detective Bortz went to #30 Pershing Lake Drive to attempt another interview with JoAnn Notheis and Jim Williams. When they rang the doorbell, Mindy answered the door and told them that her mother had gone to see an attorney. Being suspicious, the detectives waited at the top of the hill and watched the residence. A short while later they saw a GMC pickup truck pull into the Notheis' driveway. It was Jim. JoAnn, Bryan, and Mindy quickly exited the front door, climbed into the truck, and they drove off.

When a member of the Major Case Squad called JoAnn that evening, she told him that both her and Jim's attorney advised them not to answer any more questions. She then hung up.

A few days later the police became even more suspicious of Jim and JoAnn being responsible for Walter's disappearance when they learned that Jim and his son, Brett, went to an auto dealership and Jim bought JoAnn a new 1984 Chrysler Laser. Walter had been missing only a week.

▪ ▪ ▪

When Bob and Diana DeAngelis found out that Walter vanished, they were shocked. They knew their good friend had had marital difficulties, but not to the point of running off without telling his parents.

Several weeks passed. Still no word. To add to their concern, when DeAngelis called Kay, she told him about JoAnn and Jim, and the strong suspicions she and her husband had about their involvement with Walter's disappearance. That was when the DeAngelises decided to take two thousand dollars out of their savings and hire a private detective to go to St. Louis and further investigate Walter's case.

Warren L. Berkowitz of New York flew into St. Louis. He spoke with Simcox, with friends, neighbors, everyone he could find who knew Walter. He even interviewed JoAnn. Nothing. A week later he flew back to New York with no leads as to where the DeAngelises' good friend could be.

▪ ▪ ▪

Two weeks after Walter mysteriously disappeared, Bill Brown heard a knock on his door. When he opened it, he saw Jim.

"I'd like to know if you could help me carry some paneling upstairs?" asked Jim, pointing to JoAnn's house next door.

"Sure. What are you going to do with it?"

"I'm fixing up one of the front bedrooms and moving in it. My wife's gone, and it looks like Walter's not coming back. JoAnn really needs a man around to help her take care of things, and everyone around here knows how I feel about her and the kids. So, we thought, why not. Plus, we can both save money by sharing household expenses."

▪ ▪ ▪

Although Ray Runyon had known Jim since Jim was the electrical inspector of St. Charles County, being a police officer for many years made him suspicious of Jim's recent actions. He wondered why Jim called him in the early morning hours on December 28 and how they had so easily found Walter's missing car. Then he wondered why Jim flew up to Pennsylvania with JoAnn, and why he was now blatantly living at her house. Recently, he also had strong suspicions about how Sharon really died.

The police speculated where Walter's body might be. It couldn't be in the ground since the temperatures had been in the low teens to subzero since mid-December. Nor could it have been thrown into any ponds, lakes, or rivers, since these also had been solidly frozen for over a month.

Runyon decided to take a look around Jim's place. He searched the barn. Nothing. He walked the fields behind the home. Nothing. Although he had a gut feeling that Walter's body was hidden on the property, he couldn't find it. Runyon knew about the cistern, but years later he said he never considered it as a grave for Walter's body.

▪ ▪ ▪

In mid-January, Jim contacted Ron Tollesfrud, a carpenter. He asked him to help finish a deck he had started on his house, and also to build a flower planter over the cistern. Tollesfrud called a mutual friend, Runyon, and told him about this unusual request. He said he tried to convince Jim to wait until it warmed up, but Jim said he wanted it done right away since he was going to have a barbecue for his employees in another week. When Runyon heard this he said, "Wow! Hardy employees! They're going to freeze their asses off at that barbecue."

When Brett stopped by his dad's house a few days later, he

saw Jim, one of his dad's employees, and Tollesfrud working on the deck and cistern. Walking over to his dad, who was mixing concrete to pour over the cistern, he asked, "What are you doing?"

"Covering the cistern with a flower planter. I thought it would look nicer."

"Why now? It's so blazin' cold out."

"Well, son, you know my philosophy. Business is kinda slow and you know how I think it's important to keep all the employees going with a full day's work. So, I thought we'd get this done. By spring we'll have too much electrical work going on to get to this."

Brett also thought it was odd that when his mom was alive, she asked Jim several times to build flower planters for her, but he never had the time. Now with his mother dead only three months, his father was in the process of building one, and in the middle of winter.

As Brett looked down at the top of the cistern, he noticed his dad had placed a piece of plywood on top of the concrete lid and was now pouring concrete over the wood. He couldn't imagine why his dad was putting concrete on top of concrete.

A few days later his father had a truck bring in a load of dirt to be placed into the flower planter. He told Brett to fill in the planter. Brett ignored his request. For three weeks his father badgered him to fill it. Brett couldn't understand the urgency of doing it, and still neglected to follow his father's orders. One day as he went by the house, he saw his father busy with a shovel, filling in the planter with the dirt.

In April, Brett and his fiance, Jan, were soon to be married, and Jim rented his house to them. Right before they moved in, Jim Mitts, a carpenter in the area, nailed foot high pickets all around the flower planter. The project was done.

■ ■ ■

Kay and Walter had only received one short letter from JoAnn three weeks after she changed to an unlisted telephone number. She explained that her attorney advised her not to have contact with them. He felt her in-laws were accusatory toward her and it would be best to cease further communication.

For Easter of 1984, Kay and Walter sent Mindy and Bryan each a card with money. Although Mindy kept hers, Bryan sent his back, writing a note that he didn't need their money. Not only did their daughter-in-law terminate her relationship with them, but so did their grandchildren.

■ ■ ■

By July, 1984, all the neighbors had readily accepted Jim into their lives, easily supplanting Walter. He enjoyed keeping the yard looking nice, cutting it at various angles to give it a more plush look. He often had the neighbors over for barbecues or whiskey slushes in the evenings. And everyone knew how much he idolized JoAnn, taking her shopping and spending hundreds of dollars for an outfit or two. He also spent a lot of time with the twins, taking Bryan hunting and fishing, and Mindy bowling.

Despite Bill and Pat Brown having been friends with Walter, they liked Jim too. His gregarious personality complemented his outward appearance, and many people considered Jim a good looking man. Whenever he took JoAnn out, he enjoyed wearing stylish brand-named clothes. And usually he drew attention wherever he went because of his six foot six inch height and his confident manner of walking.

Since Jim believed in being generous to his friends, on Bill's birthday he took JoAnn, Bill, and Pat out to Brew's Restaurant in St. Charles for steak and lobster. Afterwards, he drove them to his house on Gutermuth Road. He showed them the split-level home where he and Sharon had lived, the barn and swimming pool, his new deck, and lastly, the flower planter. It was ablaze with orange and yellow marigolds. Little did the Browns' know that Walter's body floated only a few feet from them.

August, 1984–October, 1985. Through winter, spring, and summer, Jim had firmly entrenched himself in the Notheis home. Every night he came home to his surrogate family. As his love for JoAnn grew, so did his desire to have her completely to himself legally.

On August 24, 1984, JoAnn's lawyer, Eric Sowers, filed her divorce papers in St. Charles County on grounds that Walter had committed adultery, abandoned her, and had emotionally abused her. She asked for alimony and child support in her petition. Because Walter had supposedly vanished without a trace, under the law JoAnn had to post the impending divorce notification three times in the newspaper.

■ ■ ■

While Jim lived upstairs with JoAnn and the twins, John Calcaterra continued to live downstairs in his apartment. If he had suspicions about Walter's disappearance and Jim's hasty move into the household, he kept them to himself. Jim and JoAnn's father seemed to get along, but occasionally, JoAnn and her father would have an argument and they wouldn't speak for weeks. The love she had had for her mother had been profound, almost to the point of deification. She also loved her father, but they couldn't tolerate one another easily and, therefore, had frequent disputes.

In November of 1984, her father died.

John Calcaterra had been attending a performance at the Fox Theater in St. Louis with one of his lady friends. As he was driving home, he had a heart attack and died.

JoAnn was devastated. Again, life forced her to face another trauma. For days she cried, ranted in anger, and dipped into a state of depression.

"Why is this happening? Why, damnit!" she cried to Jim. "Why did Dad have to die now? My mother died of cancer, Walter disappeared, now my Dad. Everyone I've ever loved and trusted has left me."

"Come here, babe," consoled Jim, as he tried to put his arms around her and draw her near to him.

JoAnn pushed him away. "Leave me alone," she said bitterly. "Get away from me." She stalked out of the room, leaving Jim bewildered.

For days Jim said she refused to speak to him or have him touch her. It was as if she were blaming him for everyone's death.

According to Jim, a good friend of JoAnn's, "Doc" Spraul, finally came over to the house to talk to her. "JoAnn, why are you shunning Jim? What has he done?"

"I just don't want him to touch me. I want to be left alone."

"You better get your shit together. There's no man who's ever loved you as Jim does. He'd give up his life to see you happy. Don't you know that?"

JoAnn looked down at the floor.

"Do you think Walter ever loved you as much as Jim does?"

Looking up, she quietly said, "At one time he did."

"Well, Walter's not around anymore, is he?"

JoAnn started crying.

"I know it's been a rough year for you, JoAnn, but you've got to realize that you now have only your two kids and Jim. Don't shut him out. He needs you, and I know you need him, too."

After that conversation, JoAnn apologized to Jim and their life together continued.

▪ ▪ ▪

A short time after John died, Jim came home one Thursday night and announced to JoAnn, "Guess where we're going this weekend?"

"To a party?"

"Well, you could say that." He smiled at her and asked, "Who's your favorite singer?"

"You know who it is. Englebert Humperdinck." Her eyes got bigger and she said, "You mean he's coming to St. Louis?"

"No, hon. He's in Las Vegas and we're flying there tomorrow night for his midnight show."

"What? Really? Oh, you're just joking."

"Nope. I've already made the reservations."

"Jim, I don't believe it. This is unreal!" shouted JoAnn as she grabbed Jim and gave him a big hug.

Their flight arrived in Las Vegas at eleven o'clock. Jim told the cab driver he'd have an extra tip if he could get them to the MGM Hotel before the midnight show.

Because Jim used to fly out to Las Vegas at least once a month when he was married to Sharon, he had gotten to know several employees at various hotels. When they entered the theater, the maitre d' recognized Jim. Then he stared at JoAnn and smiled. "Ah, Mr. Williams, so this is the one, huh?" Jim smiled and nodded.

"See what you can do about getting us good seats," said Jim, and slipped the maitre d' a twenty dollar bill.

As they kept walking closer and closer to the stage, JoAnn's usual reticence disappeared and her grin widened. "Where is he taking us?"

"Just wait, babe. The best for you."

As they reached a table next to the stage, the maitre d' pulled out a chair for JoAnn. "Is this good enough for the young lady?"

Jim laughed as he saw a little girl look of wonderment on JoAnn's face.

"Jim, I can't believe this! It's like a fairytale. To think I'm finally going to see Englebert Humperdinck in person. And we're so close, I could probably touch him."

Once Humperdinck came on stage and began singing, JoAnn leaned over to Jim and said, "I can actually smell his cologne!"

Jim loved showing JoAnn how much he loved her. He continued to give her flowers, buy her jewelry and clothes, and take her to nice places. Although Jim was big and had rough eyes, he knew that women liked attention and softness and romance. He wanted to make sure JoAnn stayed with him for the rest of his life, and he believed that a loving relationship wasn't based on a battle of the wills, or even a fifty-fifty arrangement. According to him, to keep the love alive, a couple had to both try making life easier for the other, and to always show love and respect. Jim was the type of man who would try to do anything for this woman he loved.

▪ ▪ ▪

On October 11, 1985, as JoAnn walked into the St. Charles County Circuit Court to finalize the dissolution of her marriage to Walter, she saw Kay and Walter Notheis turn from their seats and stare at her. She immediately stopped. Then she and the friends who came with her backed out of the doorway. A few minutes later, she entered with her lawyer. Keeping her eyes focused on the judge's bench, her head up and her spine straight, she walked to the front of the courtroom. Within fifteen minutes she was no longer Walter's wife.

April 6, 1986. When Walter and JoAnn had gotten married in 1969, they went to a courthouse in St. Louis and a judge married them. After Jim and JoAnn decided to marry, Jim insisted that they have a big wedding.

Because JoAnn wanted to get married in the Catholic church, she and Jim had to have several meetings with a priest friend of Jim's, Father Tom of Saints Joachim and Ann Catholic Church on McClay Road in St. Charles County. Father Tom bowled on the same league as Jim at Harvest Bowling Lanes. He was a young priest who also performed magic tricks, loved to sing, and enjoyed an occasional beer on bowling nights.

At one of the first meetings, the priest asked Jim, "Do you and JoAnn plan on having any children?"

"Are you kidding?" asked Jim incredulously.

The priest's eyebrows went up. "No, Jim. It's an important question I ask all couples contemplating marriage."

"Well, I'll tell you, Tom, after the operation I had, I'd better not have any kids!" JoAnn looked embarrassingly at Jim, then at the priest. "Would that create a problem with our getting married in the Catholic church?"

The priest cleared his throat. "Not really. Because Jim is not Catholic and he had this operation performed prior to meeting you and your decision to marry, it won't prevent you from getting married in church. It's just that if you were planning to have children, I wanted to know if he would raise your offspring in the Catholic faith."

Jim smiled. "If I had met this wonderful lady when I was younger and before I had a vasectomy, I'd love to have had several children with her. And if she wanted them raised Catholic, I'd have no problem with that, Tom."

After a few more meetings, Jim and JoAnn excitedly looked forward to April 6.

▪ ▪ ▪

On the morning of their wedding day, both awoke with churning stomachs and racing hearts. Both felt like young lovers getting married for the first time, not a forty-seven year old man and a forty year old woman, each having experienced a previous marriage.

JoAnn insisted on adhering to tradition and would not allow Jim to see her until she came down the aisle. Relatives and neighbors came over early. The women heading upstairs to help JoAnn get ready laughingly warned Jim his life was doomed if he even thought about putting one foot on the staircase. For over an hour he listened to a multitude of women's voices chattering and giggling as JoAnn dressed. Occasionally he heard someone say, "Damn these buttons!" The entire back of JoAnn's three-quarter length dress contained a row of thirty tiny buttons.

Over three hundred guests filled the church. Jim hadn't seen JoAnn since the night before. In a small room to the side of the altar, his best man, who was his son, Brett, joked with his father, trying to calm him down. Soon, the organ music began and the soloist started singing. Someone opened the door. "We're ready. Time to get out there."

As Jim stood in his tuxedo in front of the altar, he looked around the church, smiling and nodding to people he knew. Few people could tell how nervous he was. Then the organist began playing "The Wedding March." Everyone turned to see Mindy, JoAnn's maid of honor, walk down the aisle. Jim gave her a wink as she glanced at him. Then in came JoAnn.

Jim's eyes welled up as he saw her walking slowly toward him. Everyone stood up and smiled at JoAnn's glowing radiance. Her large wide-brimmed hat set off her dark Italian eyes, which now emitted love and warmth, not her usual wariness. Leaning over to Bryan, who walked her down the aisle, she whispered to him and they both smiled at Jim. As she joined him, they clasped hands, each feeling the other's nervousness. Later, Jim would say, "At that moment, I thought I'd died and gone to heaven."

After exchanging their marriage vows, Jim, JoAnn and their three hundred guests drove twenty miles to Yacovelli's, a popular restaurant in north St. Louis County. Instead of limiting the food and an open bar for only an hour or two, Jim told the catering manager to make sure food and free liquor would be available for the entire evening.

Once the wedding party finished eating, Jim asked the disk jockey to play "Once in My Life" by Lee Greenwood. He took JoAnn by the hand and led her onto the dance floor. As they twirled to the music, Jim looked into her eyes and sang. Since both were adept at dancing, they gracefully circled the dance floor, oblivious to the onlookers. During the first break, JoAnn, wanting to remain traditional, threw her bridal bouquet. One of her best friends and also a neighbor, Betty Kuchta, caught it.

After the reception, some friends and neighbors returned to Jim and JoAnn's house for more drinks. Jim then decided to take them for a hayride, minus the hay. Still in his tuxedo, he hooked his tractor up to his trailer bed and told everyone to pile on. He circled the Park Charles South subdivision, then went down St. Peter's Road to the Huck's convenience store for several boxes of Twinkies. On the way back a policeman stopped him because Jim hadn't connected his trailer lights. Since he knew Jim, he just gave him a warning and told him to head right home.

The sky was beginning to lighten when the last person left. Jim and JoAnn climbed the stairs, undressed and snuggled together in the large king-sized bed. No longer was Walter's picture on JoAnn's dresser. No longer did his cologne linger in the room. The man who fell in love with Walter's wife was now her legal husband.

May, 1986–February, 1987. Soon after Jim and JoAnn were married, he came home one evening and said, "You know, I've been thinking that you come home tired and need to rest, but you still have the kids and house to take care of. I'd really like to see you quit your job and stay home."

JoAnn looked up at Jim in shock. "What? Are you kidding?"

"What I mean is you don't have to work unless you want to."

"You're serious?"

"Sure am, babe. Although business isn't like it used to be, I still make enough money to support the four of us. And I'd love to see you more relaxed, not so drained at the end of the day."

JoAnn wrapped her arms around Jim's middle. "Oh, I'd love to stay home."

So, JoAnn quit her job and became a full-time homemaker. After cleaning the house, she would sometimes go shopping, one of her favorite pastimes. Occasionally, Jim would take off in the middle of the day to join her. One time after seeing a particularly nice outfit on a mannequin, he told the sales clerk that he wanted everything on it. This was not an unusual thing for Jim to do. But when the sales person told Jim that they could find the shoes on the lower level, he stopped smiling and his eyes glowered.

"You must not have understood what I just said," he stated firmly. "I told you quite clearly that I wanted everything on this mannequin, including the shoes. She wears a size eight and a half. Now, do you get my drift?"

The sales clerk nodded nervously a few times.

"Good." Then taking a one hundred dollar bill from his money clip, he said, "Don't be long."

Although many people found Jim friendly and generous, when someone didn't comply to his request or hindered his intent, his eyes could become dark, threatening. Few people pushed him beyond his ominous look.

■ ■ ■

Their marriage settled into a comfortable pattern. Jim worked; JoAnn took care of the house and shopped. On warm weekends, Jim would cut the grass Saturday mornings. After JoAnn cleaned the house, she would join him by the lake where he would fish. They'd sit on the bank, sipping coffee while quietly talking. Sometimes the twins would join them, especially Bryan, who enjoyed fishing next to Jim.

When Jim first met JoAnn, he got along well with her children, but he noticed how spoiled they were. They knew how to keep after her until they got what they wanted. Jim thought because Walter was never around to both actively love and discipline them that JoAnn felt sorry for the twins and gave into their demands. Besides Bryan being hyperactive and Mindy having a quick temper, Jim added that both were strong-willed and sometimes rude.

Jimi, Jr., and Brett knew what a firm disciplinarian their father was. If they disobeyed him or lied or came home with bad grades, Jim would take off his belt or grab a piece of electrical wire and whip them.

After he and JoAnn were married, Jim kept a wooden paddle on a kitchen shelf. He had told Bryan that if he ever came home with a failing grade, he would get a spanking.

One day Jim came home early and JoAnn was gone. When Bryan walked in the door from school, he immediately saw Jim and tried to hide a piece of paper.

"What's that?" asked Jim.

"Nothing."

"You sure are trying to hide a piece of 'nothing' pretty fast, aren't you?"

"No, it's okay."

Jim raised an eyebrow. "It's your report card, isn't it?"

"Yeah. I'll show it to Mom when she gets home."

"Let me see it," demanded Jim, holding out his hand.

"No. It's for my Mom to see, not you. You're not my dad."

Bryan then heard JoAnn coming in the front door and ran to her. As she came into the kitchen, Jim told her about Bryan trying to hide his report card. Bryan handed it to his mother. As she read it, she pressed her lips firmly together and slightly shook her head.

"Let me see it, babe."

JoAnn hesitated for a few seconds, then handed it to Jim. After taking a look, he stared at Bryan, who stood close to his mother, and said, "I think you get three licks with this paddle."

"No, listen, I'll study harder."

"That wasn't the deal, was it? You said you'd bring up your grades last time, and you didn't uphold your end of the bargain. For that, you get three whacks on your butt."

"Mom, he can't whip me. He's not my dad, he's only my step-dad."

JoAnn took a deep breath, looked at Jim, then back at Bryan. "Jim's right. He told you what he would do if you continued to bring home bad grades." She turned and walked out of the room.

For four or five days Bryan didn't speak to Jim. But the next weekend Jim asked the fourteen year old if he wanted to join him and another friend for two days of fishing at Mark Twain Lake. The silence ended.

■ ■ ■

Although the police didn't have Walter's body as evidence that he was murdered, they continued to believe that Jim and JoAnn were responsible for his disappearance. They searched everywhere. They even called in psychics to locate Walter's whereabouts. Nothing. And despite the attending physician at the hospital signing Sharon Williams' death certificate as injuries due to an automobile accident, some police officers and paramedics who were on the scene felt differently. Because Jim had started spending the night at Walter's home the night after Walter disappeared, his wife's death became more suspect.

In October of 1986, a man died in a head-on collision after slamming into a utility pole in St. Charles County. At first authorities thought he had died due to injuries sustained from the accident. But when Dr. Mary Case, the recently appointed Chief Medical Examiner for St. Charles County, performed an autopsy on him, she determined that he had died from a gunshot wound, a victim of a cross-country murderous rampage by Michael Wayne Jackson.

Because Sharon Williams never had an autopsy, and there were strong suspicions regarding her accident, St. Charles County Sheriff, Edward Uebinger, spoke to Case on October 13, 1986, and asked if she would be willing to review the files and reports concerning Sharon's death. She agreed.

On October 28, 1986, Case called Uebinger. "Sheriff, I've gone over the police reports, the hospital records, and the death certificate on Sharon Williams, and it's my opinion that her death is most likely not from head injuries resulting from the accident. Instead, I strongly believe they were caused by multiple blunt trauma impacts to the head."

"That's what I thought, too. The accident was too minor to result in her type of injury."

"I believe that an autopsy would be definitive in terms of revealing how injuries to her head had been made."

"That might present a problem. Her husband is who we suspect, and we don't want him to know about an autopsy on his former wife. He might skip town if he had to sign the consent papers to have his wife exhumed."

"Sheriff, I've performed some autopsies where a body had to be exhumed, and a parent or child of the deceased signed the consent papers."

"That's a consideration. Listen, Mary, if I schedule a meeting for next week, can you come over to my office and discuss this with my staff?"

"I'm looking at my appointment book and see that I'll have some time available on November 4."

"Great! Thanks a lot. I really appreciate your time and assistance."

"No problem. I'm glad to help you with this."

Three days later, Case wrote Charles Garnati, the state attorney at Williamson County in Marion, Illinois, requesting permission for Sharon Williams' exhumation. Unfortunately, Garnati didn't want to get involved. When Case spoke to him on the telephone, he told her, "It's no concern of mine." Even when Sheriff Uebinger and the St. Charles County counselor, Daniel G. Pelikan, called Garnati, Garnati's secretary told him that Garnati was unavailable but would call back. No phone calls were ever returned.

After numerous attempts to contact Garnati, Attorney Pelikan, who was licensed to practice law in Illinois as well as Missouri, finally spoke with the Illinois state attorney. The conversation was brief. Garnati told Pelikan he didn't have the time. The legal maneuvers to exhume Sharon's body without Jim's permission were just beginning.

■ ■ ■

After living in Walter and JoAnn's house for three years, Jim decided to put his own home on market. He contacted Scott Peterson of Gundaker Realty. Jim's large lot, barn, pool, and home listed for over one hundred fifty thousand dollars in December of 1986.

As he walked around his property with the realtor, he pointed to the flower planter. "I put that in about three years ago. My wife always wanted one. It's sort of in memory of her."

Peterson looked at Jim and shook his head in sympathy at Jim's loss. "It's hard to get on with your life when you lose someone you really love."

Jim stared down at the planter. "You're right. But I just remarried this year. Found a wonderful woman and I'm very happy."

"You're lucky. Most men drown their grief in whiskey and wild women. Then they're sort of stuck in a rut."

"Not me. I knew I loved her the first day I saw her." Then Jim pointed down to the planter. "I think you ought to know there's a cistern under there."

"Where?"

"Under the planter. We only used it for watering the grass and washing the cars and trucks. Not much use for anything else. But I thought you should know about it."

"Sure. Let me jot that down. Won't be of any use to the new owners, but I guess it won't hurt for them to know about it."

■ ■ ■

In February, Jim's business had slowed down considerably. He had also discovered that Brett and some of his other employees were ripping him off.

Jim stated that besides his son working for him during the day, at night six foot ten Brett was a bouncer at the Brass Spur, a popular nightspot in St. Charles. Brett's wife, Jan, worked in Jim's office as his secretary. If Jim would be around the shop, Brett would stay home and catch up on his sleep. Then if Jim left, Jan would call Brett to wake him up and tell him to get over to the job site. At the time Brett earned close to seven hundred dollars a week as an electrician.

Jim also noticed that his gas bill at the Phillips 66 station where he had a business account had been steadily increasing. One day he stopped by the station to talk to the manager about it. She told Jim that when his workers filled up the trucks, they also filled up their arms with cases of soda and cupcakes. After Jim told her that only gas for his electrical trucks should be charged to his account, not food or anything else, the bill dropped by several hundred dollars.

But it wasn't until a short time later when Jim drove up to one of his jobs that his ire kicked in. As he pulled into a new residential area he had been contracted to wire, he saw several of his work crew, Brett among them, sitting on the back of a pickup tailgate and laughing as they threw mudballs against the side of the newly built house. As soon as they saw him, they jumped off and backed away. Jim yelled and cursed and threatened to fire them.

That night he went home and talked to JoAnn about it. "I've reached a point where I'm tired of putting out all this money in their wages and not getting much of a return. The last few months business has been real bad. I think I'm going to lay off everyone tomorrow."

"What about us? Can you make enough on your own?"

"No problem. If I just work by myself, I can easily make from four to five hundred a day. Do you think you can live on that?"

"Sure."

"Good. I'm tired of all this shit Brett and the other guys are giving me. If they want to treat me like shit, I can make it shittier for them."

The next day he laid everyone off, including his son.

■ ■ ■

In a police report, Brett stated that after his mother's death, he saw a marked change in his father's personality. Within two weeks from his mother's burial, his father no longer expressed grief or loneliness. Brett told the officer that he thought that was strange, especially since his parents had been married over twenty-five years. And since his father became involved with JoAnn, he no longer associated with old friends of the family.

When Jim laid Brett and the other workers off, he told them the business was becoming too much of a burden and it was getting more difficult to run. Brett didn't agree. He said that his father liked to boast about how much money he had spent on JoAnn or her kids. And in February, Jim had begun to remodel JoAnn's house. Brett stated to one of the detectives that he believed JoAnn manipulated his father, and that whatever JoAnn wanted, JoAnn got.

The man Brett used to idolize was now like a stranger to him. And the suspicions he felt about his mother's death and Walter Scott's disappearance steadily mounted over the three year period. His brother, Jimi, who was in prison in Florida, agreed. He told Brett that eventually the truth would come out.

■ ■ ■

In February of 1987, ten months after they had gotten married, Jim took JoAnn on a honeymoon cruise to the Virgin Islands. Although he laid off all of his employees and money was tighter, he had promised JoAnn this trip months before. Their good friend and neighbor, Betty Kuchta, and her fiance were also joining them. She had asked Jim and JoAnn to be best man and maid of honor at her wedding on one of the islands.

After docking at St. Thomas, JoAnn helped Betty into her own wedding dress, patiently buttoning all thirty tiny buttons down the back. Betty even wore JoAnn's wide-brimmed hat.

Their long week in the sun, the warmth, and the balmy breezes quickly ended as they landed to the bitterly cold St. Louis temperatures. Within a few weeks they would also only have memories of what it was like to be together in a settled life without jails, lawyers, TV crews, and reporters.

April 1–April 10, 1987. Early in the morning on April 1, 1987, Dr. Mary Case, Attorney Dan Pelikan, Lt. Peggy Neer, and Sgt. Donald Messner left St. Louis and drove to Marion, Illinois. Two and a half hours later they arrived at Mitchell-Hughes Funeral Home. First, they met with Larry Hughes, the funeral director, to talk about the procedures of the exhumation. Next, they all had a lengthy discussion with Sharon's mother and brother, Alice and Roy Almaroad.

The three law officials laid out their reasons for suspecting that Sharon was murdered, and quite possibly by her former husband. Case then tried to explain in terms that a lay person could comprehend why she strongly believed Sharon did not die from the minor auto accident. Mrs. Almaroad dearly loved her daughter and remembered the deep closeness they had had for forty-three years.

"I know this is painful for you, Mrs. Almaroad, but we can't prove anything without exhuming your daughter's body and doing an autopsy. Would you give us your permission?" asked Case.

"You know, I've always felt something wasn't right about how Sharon died. Sharon suspected Jim was having an affair. I tried to soften things for her and told her it probably wasn't so. But inside here," Mrs. Almaroad said, pointing to her heart, "I felt he was. And after her funeral when he wouldn't come back to my house for the reception, I thought that was real odd. Then I heard he was already mixed up with this JoAnn person and that she sorta took over his life. I only know he sure changed. Maybe this autopsy will put the pieces together."

After Mrs. Almaroad signed the consent forms, Case and the police officers then proceeded to Fountain United Methodist Cemetery where three employees of the Doric Vault Company uncovered the earth on top of the concrete vault. They then transported the casket with Sharon's remains to the St. Louis County Morgue.

■ ■ ■

The next day Case performed the autopsy on Sharon Williams' body. Lt. Neer and Detectives Cover and Luetkenhaus of the St. Charles County Sheriff's office arrived to take pictures.

The morgue attendants placed the body on the examination table. Sharon wore a long peach negligee. Beneath this, from her neck down to her ankles, she was encased in a white plastic body suit. Besides the negligee, a bra, panties, and white socks, the only other article on her body was a gold cross attached to a gold chain.

After Case took various measurements of the body, she looked for scars or other body markings, like tattoos or wounds. Externally, the body was well preserved for being buried since 1983. Anyone who had known Sharon would still have had recognized her.

Once Case recorded this information, she made an incision in the chest and abdomen, and thoroughly examined all the organs in these areas. Despite Sharon's death three and a half years prior to the autopsy, her stomach still contained the food she had last eaten when she and Jim went out to dinner on October 19, 1983. Case then noted that Sharon had had a hysterectomy, since there was no uterus. Although her eyes, pancreas, spleen, kidneys, and the long bones of her upper extremities had been donated upon her death, the remaining organs proved healthy.

The head was next. The medical examiner observed several abrasions, superficial lacerations, and bruises to the front of the head, all consistent with the type of accident Sharon had experienced. Most of the attention was then conducted to the back of the head, the site of the fatal injury. After making an incision into the scalp, Case examined the skull. On either side, up toward the top of the head, two deep linear wounds were noticeable. Each measured from two and a half to three inches, with a six inch gap between them. They were so deep that the underlying bone was extensively fractured.

Once Case lifted off the skull cap, she noted that the fracture extended down to the skull base. The bone had been fractured into multiple fragments. Being one of four experts in the country holding dual certification in forensic pathology and neuropathology, she knew that a bowling ball did not produce a linear laceration of this type. A hammer was also ruled out. A meat cleaver could produce a similar laceration, but the underlying bone injury would be very different. Whatever caused Sharon's injury had to have had a linear structure, such as a lead pipe or crowbar.

She concluded that the massive, severe head injuries were inconsistent with Sharon's type of automobile accident. Manner of death: homicide.

▪ ▪ ▪

According to a police statement, at six o'clock in the morning on April 3, Jim Williams called Sharon's cousin Imogene Benton, who lived in Marion, Illinois.

"I need you to do me a favor," requested Jim. "Something's going on and I want you to go out to the cemetery. See if Sharon's grave's been messed with. Would you do that for me?"

"Sure, but what do you think's going on?"

"Don't know for sure, but yesterday the Sheriff called Brett in to question him about Sharon's death. And things are just coming down on me right now. Business is real bad. I had to lay everyone off, including Brett. And he just got a divorce. It's so bad that I may have to file bankruptcy. It's been one hell of a year."

"It's been a long time since we've seen or heard from you, Jim. At least a year."

"I know. Just lots going on here. Anyway, I'd appreciate it if you'd head out to the cemetery now and check on this for me."

"Okay. I'll call you when I get back."

Three hours later she called him. "You're right, Jim. The grave's dug up. There's no casket in it at all."

"Shit! I don't know what's going on, but I'm sure in the hell going to find out."

"Jim, I want to ask you something." She hesitated a moment, then asked, "Did you have anything to do with Sharon's death?"

"No, Imogene, I did not. Gotta go. Thanks for going out to the cemetery."

▪ ▪ ▪

Late in the afternoon Jim called his friend, Ray Runyon of the St. Charles County Sheriff's office. "Ray, what in the hell is going on?"

"What do you mean, Jim?"

"They dug up Sharon's grave. There's no casket. Nothing in it. They can't dig her up unless I give them my permission. I'm next of kin. And the detectives called Brett in to talk to them. Find out what the fuck's going on, will you?"

"I have no idea what's happening. Have you called your attorney?"

"No. Guess I need to give him a call. Meanwhile, keep your ears opened. Find out what kind of shit they're going to try to nail me with."

■ ■ ■

Several days later, Sgt. Norm Forgue, a member on Jim's bowling league, received a call from another policeman on the team.

"Norm, Rudi Meyers here. Hey, Big Jim can't make it tonight. Can you sub for him?"

"Why? What's going on? Jim never misses."

"I know. It seems like his former in-laws are creating some problems. Someone's dug up Sharon's grave. He thinks they may try to pin something on him."

"Whew, you're kidding?"

"Nope. And JoAnn's ex-in-laws are accusing them of killing their son."

"Sounds like he's in a shitload of trouble."

"Yep. I heard this from Frank Biffiriano. He's really pissed at Jim, too. I can't blame him. Here the guy goes on vacation, comes back to the job, and Jim gives him no notice at all. Just tells him he's laid off."

Forgue said, "Did you know Biffiriano's girlfriend is good friends with Jim's new wife, JoAnn? I wonder how this will affect that friendship. This should all prove interesting."

Forgue had only known JoAnn for a year, but already she had become fairly good friends with him and his wife. On bowling nights at Harvest Lanes, he and JoAnn talked quite a bit. The next time he saw JoAnn, he would ask her what was going on.

■ ■ ■

Once the autopsy had been performed and Case determined that Sharon's death was a homicide, two detectives, Steve Roach and Walter Blankenship, of the St. Louis Major Case Squad, flew down to Key West, Florida, to interview Jimi Williams, who was back in prison for another offense.

When they told him of the autopsy's findings, he became extremely agitated. Because Jim had asked his son to rough someone up over Christmas of 1983 for five hundred dollars, they thought he might know about Walter Scott's disappearance.

"Jimi, do you have any idea where Scott's body might be?"

"Let's see. The weather was pretty cold, right? So, it couldn't be put in the ground or in a lake or river. You checked my old man's barn already?"

The two men nodded.

"What about the cistern?"

The detectives' stomachs lurched. But outwardly, they kept a cool exterior. "What cistern are you talking about, Jimi?"

"The one behind the house on Gutermuth. It would be the perfect place to hide a body."

"Do you know anything about the murder?"

"Might. If you can get me out of this hole and back up to Missouri or Illinois, I can give you information that could help you. But if there's no deal, I don't talk. Understand?"

"Did you murder Walter Scott?"

"I've done lots of things against the law, but I ain't no murderer. Understand?" Jimi stared at them without any sign of emotion. "Now, want to cut a deal?"

"Don't know, Jimbo. We have to talk with our boss when we get back."

"Let me know if you find Scott's body in the cistern. If you do, just remember who told you where it was. And if you want more information, I want something out of it. Clear?"

▪ ▪ ▪

After the detectives returned to St. Charles, they again interviewed Brett Williams. Initially when they began to question him, the detectives reported that it was difficult for Brett to tell them about his father's behavior and about his strong suspicions that Jim was connected to the murders. Yet once he realized that his father was probably responsible for their deaths, he cooperated.

When they questioned him about where he thought Jim might have put Walter's body, like his older brother, he surmised the ground was too frozen to dig a grave the night Walter disappeared. And with the sub-zero temperatures St. Louis had experienced, most lakes and rivers were ice-packed. But, he told the detectives, his father did have a cistern on his property. It seemed the most likely place to stash a body.

With the information provided by Jim's sons, the Sheriff's department prepared a search warrant. On April 10, 1987, Associate Circuit Judge William Lohmar, signed a search warrant at six-eighteen in the evening to authorize a search of James H. Williams's premises at 5647 Gutermuth Road. It stated it was for the express purpose of locating the body of Walter Notheis, also known as "Walter Scott." The warrant even specifically stated the main area to be searched: the cistern at the rear of the house, covered by a wooden flower planter.

After the police officials retrieved Walter's body from the cistern and opened up the sealed plastic bag, which contained several of his credit cards and his driver's license, Simcox called two of his detectives on his police phone. "Okay, guys, take him into custody. We've got the body."

▪ ▪ ▪

Detectives Stan Lucas and Bill Presson pulled up in front of the brick and frame two-story house in the Park Charles South subdivision, walked up to the porch and pressed the doorbell. The original owner of the house had just been found in the cistern. The door opened.

"Jim Williams?"

"Yeah, that's me."

"I'm Detective Lucas and this is my partner, Detective Presson, of the St. Charles County Sheriff's office. I guess you know why we're here?"

"Nope, don't have a clue."

"May we come in?"

"Sure, just ripping up the living room carpet, so excuse the mess."

They entered the foyer and Lucas said, "We're here to arrest you on suspicion of the capital murders of your former wife, Sharon Williams, and of Walter Notheis, Jr. We just found his body in the cistern behind your house on Gutermuth."

"Don't know nothin' about it," Jim responded quietly.

"Sorry, Mr. Williams, but we think you do and we're taking you in." Lucas proceeded to read Williams the Miranda rights.

At this time JoAnn came into the foyer, her brown eyes wide in disbelief, her mouth firmly set. "What's going on?"

Jim took her hand, drawing her closer. "Don't worry, babe. Everything will be all right. Call Wolff and tell him about this."

He took JoAnn into his arms, and closing his eyes tightly, embraced her for several seconds. After Jim audibly whispered into her ear that he loved her, Detective Presson handcuffed him. JoAnn's eyes filled with confusion and fear as she watched the two detectives take her husband to the county jail.

■ ■ ■

After the police left with Jim, Don Wolff, a prominent St. Louis defense attorney, stated that JoAnn called him. Shaking and crying, she told him about Jim's arrest.

In his deep, booming voice he told her, "JoAnn, calm down and listen to me. You may also be a strong suspect in Walter's murder, and the police may be issuing a warrant for your arrest at this very moment. I want you to leave the house immediately. Go to a relative's or a good friend's house and stay put.

I'll begin arrangements to get a bond set in case they want to take you into custody."

"I can't leave yet. Mindy's out with some friends and I'm not sure where she is."

"JoAnn, you've got to go now. Some neighbors can take care of her until we have things more under control. Can you think of somewhere you can stay for a few days?"

"I think so. God, Don, I'm so scared."

"I know you are, but everything will be okay. Just get the hell out of the house and give me a call as soon as you get to where you'll be staying."

"Will I have to go to jail?"

"If you do, it won't be for long. Maybe only a day or two. Once I get this bond thing situated, I'll have to surrender you. But don't worry, everything will be fine. Now get going."

JoAnn called Judy Steiner, one of her best friends who lived in Florissant. She told her about her predicament and that she needed a place to stay for a few days. Judy assured her that she and her husband would assist her in any way they could.

Betty Kuchta Loui, her good friend and neighbor, said JoAnn then called her. Again, JoAnn related what was going on and that she didn't feel she could drive the twenty miles to the Steiner's. Betty told her she'd drive her over.

Grabbing a few articles of clothing, her purse, and her fourteen year old son, Bryan, she dashed out of the door. According to Betty, by this time JoAnn was becoming hysterical. Betty and another neighbor firmly gripped each side of JoAnn's arms and shoved her into the front seat of Betty's car. Hurrying out of the driveway and up the street, Betty took the back way out of the subdivision.

▪ ▪ ▪

April 11, 1987. With the x-rays from the December 20, 1983, visit to his dentist, Dr. Mary Case officially identified the body as Walter Notheis, Jr., also known as Walter Scott. During the autopsy, Case tried to determine how Walter was murdered. It didn't take long. Chest x-rays revealed that he had sustained a gunshot wound to the chest area. His particular wound showed a lead snowstorm pattern, meaning that a bullet had entered his body and had exploded into tiny fragments.

Case then examined the top of the jogging suit which Walter had been wearing for over three years in the cistern. Holding it up to a light, she saw a round hole on the left shoulder, near the middle of the back. It was consistent with the gunshot wound. Because all of the skin and muscle on the body had fallen off, exposing the bones, it was impossible to see any bullet pathway.

The manner of death: homicide.

▪ ▪ ▪

After two days of hiding at the Steiner house, Don Wolff finally surrendered his client to the St. Charles County Sheriff's office. On April 12, 1987, JoAnn Marie Williams was charged with the capital murder of her ex-husband, Walter. Three days later she left her small cell after posting a five hundred thousand dollar bond. Her husband, Jim, remained jailed without bond.

April 10, 1987–September, 1987. After their son vanished, the three years, three months passed slowly for Kay and Walter Notheis, and hope dwindled that their older son would be found alive. They had made numerous calls throughout the country to people who had known Wally. No leads. They had called the St. Charles County Sheriff's department several times a week. Nothing. And they had prayed daily, as had a multitude of family members and friends. But even prayers could not remove the black weight burdening their hearts.

When the police finally uncovered the hidden cistern in Jim Williams' back yard, revealing Walter's body, Walter's parents fluctuated between sorrow and relief. Kay said, "Only a parent who has gone through this could actually know how we felt not knowing where our child was or what happened to him. I always thought he was buried in the woods. Although we felt relief in finding Wally's body, having a child of yours murdered is something you can never get over."

On April 10, 1987, Doris, Walter's first wife, was fixing her hair to go out when she heard the news bulletin on television about finding her ex-husband's body. In less than a minute, her older son called, "Mom, do you really think that's my dad they've found?"

At first Walter's two older sons didn't want to talk about it. Later, when they opened up about their father's murder, they couldn't believe how someone had gotten him into a precarious situation. They remembered him as always being so cautious, street-smart, and they knew that wherever he went, he carried a gun.

Ronnie, Walter's brother, was shocked. He said if anyone had come after Wally, the assailant would be the one beaten near death or the one shot, not his brother. Ronnie's shock turned to intense anger and bitterness. He wanted the people involved with Walter's death to pay.

On April 16, 1987, Walter Simon Notheis, Jr., was entombed in a St. Louis mausoleum. Eleven days later a memorial Mass for Walter was held at Seven Holy Founders Catholic Church in Affton, Missouri.

■ ■ ■

Discovery of Walter's body stayed in the forefront of all the news media as pictures of Jim's and JoAnn's arrests splashed across the front pages of newspapers and magazines. Reporters clamored police headquarters demanding further information. Some reporters even targeted the two younger children of Walter and JoAnn. They stood outside the school that the twins attended, taking pictures of them and hounding them for interviews.

Mindy and Bryan were confused by their father's death, wondering who murdered him and why. Family friend, Betty Loui, said they were also bewildered at the onslaught of calloused questions posed by rude reporters. Not only were the media apathetic about their feelings, but their classmates also asked offensive questions and made jeering remarks. The only safe haven for them seemed to be behind the closed doors of their home. But even amid familiar objects lurked the fear that perhaps their mother, who was out on bail, would have to return to jail. They had lost their father. They didn't want to lose their mother also, their only source of love and stability.

▪ ▪ ▪

After JoAnn's arrest for first-degree murder in connection with the death of her ex-husband, she spent three days in jail. Many of her friends posted her five hundred thousand dollar bond with their real estate, and she was released. Associate Judge William T. Lohmar ordered Jim held without bond on two murder charges: for the beating death of his first wife, Sharon Williams, and the fatal shooting of Walter Notheis, Jr.

Prior to Jim's and JoAnn's murder charges, Donald L. Wolff gave both of them legal advice. But he told them, "In the event there would be an issuance against the two of you, I couldn't represent both of you." Therefore, Wolff represented JoAnn, and he recommended that Jim contact Michael A. Turken, a respected St. Charles attorney.

Once the police released JoAnn, Wolff insisted she not visit or speak to Jim. Wolff felt his client was in a vulnerable position. To continue seeing the man charged with her ex-husband's murder might infer complicity. He thought once more evidence could be produced, he would review his position of whether or not JoAnn should have contact with her husband.

Although Wolff advised JoAnn to stay away from Jim, the twins had frequent contact with their step-father. Almost every night, Mindy or Bryan would talk to him on the phone. When JoAnn drove her children to the jail to visit Jim, he would see her standing on the parking lot looking at him, but she would not go near the building.

One time when he called the house to talk to Mindy, JoAnn answered. "I shouldn't be talking to you, Jim."

"This is bullshit! Do you know how much I miss you? Do

you know what I'm going through?"

"I know. I miss you, too. The kids miss you and so do all the neighbors."

"Being locked up like this, away from you and the twins, not free to do what I want, is eating me up inside. This is like a nightmare. I gotta get out soon."

"I know. Even though I'm not in jail, my whole life is upside down."

"How's the money situation?"

"Not good. I'm cleaning a few houses, so I'm making a little money."

"That's bullshit!" yelled Jim. "I don't want no wife of mine to go around cleaning the shit out of other people's toilets."

JoAnn became quiet, then said, "I better go. Here's Mindy."

▪ ▪ ▪

A few months after her arrest, JoAnn called Norm Forgue and asked if she could come over to his house to talk to him and his wife. He then contacted his superiors in the Sheriff's office and told them about the impending visit.

When JoAnn arrived, Forgue noticed dark circles under her eyes, and age lines etched across her forehead and around her mouth. After a few minutes of light talk, JoAnn began speaking about the night Walter had disappeared.

"When Walter left to go to Bruce's garage, I went over to a neighbor's for a short time. When I got back, Walter hadn't come home. So, I called the garage, but no one answered the phone. Then I called Bruce's wife and talked to her. Half an hour later Bruce calls me and says Walter never arrived."

"Why did Walter have to go to Bruce's that night?" asked Forgue.

"To get an inspection sticker for the car. Bruce doesn't do inspections, but he has a friend who does. It's illegal, but even some of the cops know he does this and let it go. Supposedly, he had the paperwork done up and everything was ready that night. Well, three weeks went by and I had completely forgotten about the sticker, when Bruce calls up and tells me to pick up the inspection since the license was due."

"So you picked it up several weeks after Walter disappeared?"

"No, my dad did. But another thing I don't understand is why Bruce wasn't fully investigated. Why would Bruce sell a lucrative business two years ago and move down to the Ozarks? It doesn't make sense. Where was he when I tried calling that night? He knows what happened to Walter, but he's not talking."

After JoAnn left, two officers who taped the conversation in Forgue's basement came up and undid the wires under Forgue's shirt. Although he felt uncomfortable taping the conversation without JoAnn's knowledge, he had weighed the situation carefully. His new friend of less than a year needed someone to talk to. Yet he only knew her from the bowling alley one night a week. On the other hand, he had his oath of office and his loyalty to the department and the community. He took this seriously. Therefore, he felt his duty definitely belonged with the law.

Because Sgt. Forgue was not a member of the Major Case Squad assigned to investigate this case, he was unaware of who had or had not been investigated and other details surrounding the murders. He did learn that when the police thoroughly searched the car on January 3, 1984, less than a week after Walter's disappearance, it already had a new inspection sticker on the windshield. He also learned that when Schone had been questioned, he became defensive. Soon, upon advice of his attorneys, Schone refused to answer any further questions. And now Forgue began questioning JoAnn's honesty about what actually happened on the night when Walter disappeared.

October, 1987–January, 1988. Before Walter's death, Bruce Schone's automotive business thrived. People found him affable, always smiling and ready with a new joke. Because he did the maintenance work on all of Walter's vehicles, Walter frequently visited the garage. Since JoAnn occasionally came in with Walter, and later used the garage as a meeting place for Jim, she too knew Schone. Similarly, Jim Williams took his cars and trucks into Schone's garage. And when Schone had briefly owned a tavern, he had gotten to know both of Jim's sons, Jimi, Jr., and Brett. Several deputies from the Sheriff's department also brought their personal cars into Schone's shop, including Ray Runyon.

In 1985, when Schone sold his business and moved to the Lake of the Ozarks, many of his clients wondered why he had left the St. Charles area. The police also wanted to know more about his involvement in Walter's murder. After Jim and JoAnn had been charged with Walter's murder, the police sent Detective Butch Ifland down to speak with Schone. Because the

Sheriff's office thought Schone would be more cooperative talking to a friend, Deputy Ray Runyon accompanied Ifland.

According to Runyon, he said as soon as he saw Schone, he noticed a change. No smiles. No easy laughter. Only cold steely eyes met his.

"What are you doing down here?" demanded Schone.

"I wanted to see how you're doing, Bruce. And Butch wants to ask you a few questions."

"I'm not saying a damn thing."

Ifland took out a small notebook with several pages of questions. "You're not under arrest or anything, Schone. But there are a few things we want to clear up about the night Walter Scott disappeared."

"It's that damn black widow who's trying to set me up." This was a term that many people involved in the case called JoAnn.

"No one is trying to set you up, Bruce," interjected Runyon. "But there are a few spots in the investigation that aren't clicking. And one of them has to do with Walter supposedly heading to your garage, but never making it there."

"What are you doing questioning me, Ray? I thought we were friends."

"We are, Bruce. The sheriff just thought you'd talk more easily if I came along."

"Bullshit! Fuck the sheriff! Let him come down and I'll tell him the same thing I'm going to tell you, and that's nothing!"

Runyon looked away for a few seconds, then stared back at Schone. "I know how you feel. I don't want to infringe on our friendship, but Mark Lee, who's the prosecutor handling this case, also wanted me to talk to you. He said that if you were not the trigger man in Scott's death that he'd offer you immunity."

"What do you mean?"

"That if you were the one who drove the car to the airport for Jim Williams that night, you wouldn't be charged as an accomplice to the murder if you'd give us some information as to what happened."

"Stick it up your ass! I told you I don't know a fucking thing. My lawyers have informed me I don't have to say a word."

"Bruce, I wish I weren't here in this capacity, but I think you should reconsider," said Runyon.

"I'm not saying another word. Excuse me, but I need to get back to work."

A few weeks later, Runyon stated that he drove down to visit Schone as a friend, not as a law officer. After talking for a while, Schone told him the reason he was so abrupt with Runyon was that someone else, supposedly from the Sheriff's office, came down the night before and offered him immunity. Schone thought he was being set up at that point. Then when he saw Ifland and Runyon the next day and they began questioning him and also offered him immunity, he felt it violated their friendship.

■ ■ ■

On October 1, 1987, Associate Circuit Judge Lucy D. Rauch set Jim's bond at six hundred thousand dollars. Various friends and neighbors believed in Jim's innocence and pledged their property. After six months of incarceration, Jim walked out the front door of the jail, shaking hands and waving to the trustees and deputies he had gotten to know.

Again, JoAnn's attorney, Don Wolff, emphatically told his client to keep away from her husband. For a few days she acquiesced to his demands. But since Jim moved in with one of their neighbors in Park Charles South, the temptation to see one another overrode their legal concerns. Because they knew they were under police surveillance, at first they would sneak across the back yards. After a week, they were openly living together.

Jim's electrical business had collapsed. Once he left jail, he began making crafts to sell at craft shows. He also built picnic tables, which several of his friends and neighbors bought. And he spent many days in the kitchen baking chocolate chip cookies to sell as orders for birthdays and special occasions. Sometimes a local builder would call Jim to wire a house.

The shopping sprees with JoAnn and the twins ceased, as did the frequent trips to Las Vegas. Jim's money had dwindled to nothing. But his love for JoAnn continued to be the one mainstay that brought happiness to his life.

February, 1988–June, 1990. Although the St. Charles County Sheriff's department arrested both Jim and JoAnn Williams in April of 1987 for murder, legal maneuverings by the defense attorneys and inertia in the judicial system prevented the case from going to trial.

Mike Turken, the dark-haired, short-bearded defense attorney for Jim, filed a motion to dismiss the charge since the search warrant proved flawed. It did not reveal the source of information as to who told the police that Walter's body could be found in the cistern. Apparently, D. Eugene Dalton, Jr., a former assistant prosecutor for St. Charles County who handled the search warrant, thought the information was in the application. And Judge Bill Lohmar also thought so when he signed it on April 10, 1987. Lohmar said that when he signed it, the police informed him that Jimi, Jr., told them Walter Notheis's body was in the cistern. He assumed the warrant included this relevant information.

The other glitch to this case focused on the legality of Sharon Williams's exhumation. Again, Turken filed a motion indicating such an exhumation was illegal, since Jim was the next of kin, not Sharon's mother. Thus, if the ruling dismissed the exhumation, the autopsy would not be allowed as evidence. If a judge ruled that both the search warrant and the exhumation were illegal, the prosecutors would have no legal bodies to use as evidence and the case could possibly be dismissed.

Relatives and friends of both Walter Notheis, Jr., and Sharon Williams expressed anger and frustration with the legal system. Walter's brother, Ron, told the press, "This better not happen. He's dead, and whoever did it should join him."

▪ ▪ ▪

On February 9, 1988, Lincoln County, Missouri, Associate Circuit Judge Kathie B. Guyton Dudley ruled that Sharon Williams's body was illegally exhumed. If her ruling stood up in court, it meant that the autopsy evidence would be inadmissible against Jim Williams. The police and prosecutors felt their case rapidly hitting bottom. Loved ones of the two murdered victims wondered how the judicial system could blatantly dismiss this evidence and allow the murderers to walk free. Their belief in justice prevailing in America quickly waned.

After a brief letdown, the families insisted that the prosecutors try every tactic feasible. On March 29, 1988, once more Alice Almaroad, Brett Williams, and Ray Almaroad, Jr., signed the consent papers for another exhumation and autopsy regarding Sharon. This time they found a judge in Illinois who agreed to assist them in their effort to see that justice could legally be carried out. Judge Robert H. Howerton of Williamson County signed and filed an order on April 12, 1988, to exhume the body for a second autopsy. Dr. Case performed another autopsy on April 18, 1988. The evidence could now be legally admitted.

Simultaneously, on April 15, 1988, Circuit Judge Lester W. Duggan, Jr., authorized a grand jury to be convened. A grand jury consists of twelve to twenty-three people who meet privately in a closed session to determine whether or not there's enough evidence against the person or persons to warrant a bill of indictment. It would be the first time in ten years that a St. Charles judge had found cause to have such a jury.

▪ ▪ ▪

Despite some breakthroughs in the legal chess game, Kay and Walter Notheis drove across the Blanchette Bridge from St. Louis to St. Charles several times a week. Many law officials said it was the couple's diligent efforts that kept the case alive. They either visited the Sheriff's department and talked to Lt. Wes Simcox who headed the Major Case Squad's investigation, or they went to the large-domed courthouse to check the status of the case. Attorneys who had nothing to do with the legal proceedings in this case even knew Kay and Walter by name.

One day an attorney saw Kay and Walter entering the courthouse and said, "Are you here again?"

Kay, a spunky woman who isn't afraid to speak her mind, responded, "Do you want to know something? If I thought it would do me any good, I'd take off all my clothes and get on top of this dome just to get some attention so this case gets to court."

The lawyer laughed and said, "Let me know ahead of time so I can be here to watch you."

Besides frequenting the courthouse and police headquarters, Kay and Walter appeared on several nationally televised programs to speak about their son's murder and the delay in getting the case to trial. Two of the shows were "Inside Edition" and "Hard Copy."

▪ ▪ ▪

Nine months after Jim's release from the St. Charles County jail, he was back in. So was JoAnn. On June 21, 1988, the grand jury returned indictments against both of them. But their incarcerations proved short-lived. After only a few days of being locked up, both were back at home on Pershing Lake Drive. JoAnn posted a five hundred thousand dollar bond; Jim, seven hundred fifty thousand dollars.

March, 1990–October, 1990. Almost three years after the police retrieved Walter's decomposed body from the cistern in back of Jim Williams's house and arrested Jim and JoAnn on murder charges, a trial still was not in sight. In fact, the defense attorneys, Turken and Wolff, continued to diligently file motions to dismiss the case.

In March of 1990, both filed motions to quash the grand jury indictments against Jim and JoAnn. The attorneys claimed the grand jurors were improperly selected. They argued that the jury should have been chosen by the jury commission, not the sheriff. Kent Fanning, the fourth assistant prosecutor to handle this case, upheld the selection. "The entire process, which selected the members in a purely mechanical random method, did not violate statutory and constitutional provisions for equal protection and due process."

Another defense tactic Turken and Wolff tried to take was their claim that Judge Lester W. Duggan, Jr., who had called the grand jury, should have disqualified himself. Apparently, at one time his son had been a member of Walter Scott's band. The defense argued that this gave the appearance of impropriety. Circuit Court Judge Fred Rush told the defense attorneys and the assistant prosecutor, Fanning, that he would study all their motions until their memoranda were filed.

▪ ▪ ▪

In May, 1990, the Pulitzer Publishing Company, which publishes the St. Louis Post-Dispatch, also became involved in this case when its attorneys filed a motion to make public the names of the grand jury members. The paper argued that traditionally this information had always been made available.

For two years these names were assumed to be in a sealed file under court orders. It wasn't until a reporter from the Post-Dispatch searched the open file and discovered the names accidentally that they were finally revealed. Despite Judge Duggan ordering these names sealed, a clerk in the Circuit Clerk's office mistakenly placed them in a file open to public inspection.

When Fanning heard about this, his anger flared. "This is totally ridiculous! There's even an order saying these names are to be sealed. Just because a clerk made a mistake doesn't mean this should be public. The judge gave this order because of his concern for the safety and welfare for these grand jury members."

Immediately upon attaining the list of juror names, the Post-Dispatch called them. Although most of the members didn't mind their names being used in the paper, several did, stressing they felt concern about personal safety and threatening calls.

A few days later, the prosecuting attorney's office finally received good news. Judge Fred Rush scheduled the arraignment of Jim and JoAnn Williams after rejecting the defense motions to quash their indictments.

▪ ▪ ▪

Soon after Jim began living with JoAnn, his weight shot up from two twenty-five to well over three hundred pounds. He loved to cook. But with the pending case hanging over him, his anxiety increased, which created a nervous eating pattern.

Not only did he have to endure the legal battle to keep him a free man, but now his neighbor, Bill Brown, and he were feuding. One day he had asked Bill, "It's too dark out here. With the cops and the press hounding us, I want to make sure no one comes snooping around at night, so I thought about putting up a dusk to dawn light. The only thing is it'll be shining in your back yard also. What do you think?"

Bill drove a truck over the road and had unusual hours. Sometimes he would get up and leave at two or three in the morning, and he needed undisturbed sleep. "If it doesn't bother me, no problem."

After Jim installed the light, Bill couldn't sleep well with the brightness shining into his bedroom. He told Jim about it, yet the light continued to illuminate his room. His anger mounted when Jim repeatedly ignored his requests to get rid of the light or move it elsewhere. One day he walked into the kitchen while JoAnn sat talking to his wife and said, "That no-good Jim won't do anything about turning that damn light off." With that statement, the closeness between him and JoAnn ceased, and she never spoke to Bill again.

Soon, a fence went up between the two houses. Then Jim and Bill proceeded to aggravate each other by either running a weedeater or a chainsaw close to each other's bedroom window at various times, day or night.

With the stress of being excessively overweight, the impending trial, and now the ongoing feud with his next door neighbor, Jim began having heart problems. When he and JoAnn were arraigned on June 5, 1990, he could not personally attend. A few days prior to the arraignment, Jim had undergone heart surgery. At court Joann and Jim plead not guilty to the murder charges. Over three years had passed since their arrests.

The next day Circuit Court Judge Fred Rush set scheduled dates when the prosecutor's office had to submit pertinent information to the defense, when all motions for both sides had to be filed and heard, and when the trial would begin. The projected trial date would be in October. But all attorneys stated they would need at least six months, probably a year, to prepare for a trial as complex as this one.

▪ ▪ ▪

Not only had the case taken a toll on Jim's heart, but Walter Notheis, Sr., also suffered heart problems. Throughout his life he had remained thin, yet he had just turned sixty-eight and the stress of dealing with his son's murder weighed heavily on him. Everyday he and Kay either made calls or drove over to St. Charles to inquire about the status of the case. One time when they asked Bill Hannah, the prosecuting attorney, how the case was coming along, he looked at them in frustration and said, "I have other cases besides your son's!"

Their son had disappeared December 27, 1983. Another three years had passed before police discovered his body in 1987. Three more years and the case still had not gone to trial. Their exasperation took its toll on both elderly parents, physically and mentally.

In 1988, when Kay had joined a support group, Parents of Murdered Children, she had urged Walter to also attend the meetings with her. The crux of the meetings focus on members talking about the emotional impact of experiencing the murders of their children. The group also receives information about laws and what to expect from the legal system.

Being a reticent and private man, for over a year Walter refused to join his wife at these monthly sessions. Finally, his heart problems escalated to life-threatening proportions, and on June 30, 1990, he had by-pass surgery.

■ ■ ■

The fall of 1990 was an election year for many county offices, one being the St. Charles County Prosecuting Attorney's office. Republican incumbent, William J. Hannah, received significant criticism in not handling Walter Scott's and Sharon Williams's murders expeditiously. The Democratic candidate, Tim Braun, worked strenuously to unseat Hannah, and used the Walter Scott murder case to his benefit.

Bandleader, Bob Kuban, remained in close contact with Walter's parents. He saw the grief and heartache they continued to endure for almost seven years. He saw the paper shuffling, the lies, the legal strategies to dismiss the murders. Like Kay and Walter, he wanted justice served. Although he had always steered away from political associations, he felt a need to help oust Hannah and assist Braun.

In October the Bob Kuban Brass Band donated all its proceeds from a fundraising dance to Braun's campaign fund. Hundreds of people attended the dance at Dyer Memorial Hall at St. Charles Borromeo Catholic Church. And in November, Braun won the election.

January, 1991–November, 1992. Two months after Tim Braun had won the election for the prosecuting attorney's office, he tried to dismiss himself from the Walter Scott/ Sharon Williams's murder trial. On January 7, 1991, he filed a motion for a special prosecutor to handle the case. His reason: he had ties to a defense witness.

While Braun served as a public defender, the brother to a former member of Walter Scott's band came into his office and stated that Jim Williams did not murder Walter. He told Braun that Walter had reneged on a nightclub contract in New Orleans; instead, he performed at a competitor's. At the time Walter didn't realize that the former club's owners had mob affiliations. The proprietors apparently became irate, and the informant said they put a contract out on Walter. A year after meeting with Braun, this prospective defense witness died of AIDS.

Don Wolff and Mike Turken fought Braun's motion because they believed there was no legitimate basis for Braun to disqualify himself. They even said they would waive the issue pertaining to the informant's statement of Jim Williams's innocence. Braun still said no. All the attorneys and judges knew the case was complicated and based mainly on circumstantial evidence. It would take an astute litigator with a solid background in law and a bulldog tenacity to win this case. Perhaps this reasoning was the basis why the defense attorneys attempted to thwart Braun's motion to dismiss himself. They knew as a recently elected prosecuting attorney, he would have difficulty winning a guilty verdict.

But Braun won his motion at the Supreme Court.

On March 1, 1991, Circuit Judge Fred Rush appointed the attorney general's office as special prosecutor. Shortly thereafter, Thomas E. Dittmeier became that special prosecutor for the case. If any attorney could overcome the arduous task of sifting through volumes of court transcripts, police investigative notes and statements, and stacks of documents on a case with so little concrete evidence and still win, it would be Tom Dittmeier.

Dittmeier, who attended the prestigious all-boys' high school in St. Louis, CBC, and later graduated from law school at St. Louis University, knew the importance of being self-disciplined and focused in attempting to overcome insurmountable undertakings. Being a former Golden Gloves championship boxer, he retained the same stamina and steadfastness when he became an attorney. And just like the picture hanging in his office of his movie hero John Wayne, Dittmeier had always been a strong advocate of law and order.

Although a court date had not been set and Dittmeier was still involved in other litigations, he did begin preliminary work on the murder case. He stated that he found Sheriff Uebinger and the co-commander of the Major Case Squad, Wes Simcox, helpful in assisting him. Their files and flow charts were organized, unlike the laxity he observed in how the prosecuting attorney's office handled the matter. He also expressed problems in getting the presiding judge, Donald E. Dalton, to respond to his letters and phone calls. But like Braun, in a few months Dalton disqualified himself on the grounds that he felt a conflict of interests since his son helped prepare the search warrant on Jim Williams's property. He requested a special judge to oversee the case.

On December 10, 1991, the Missouri Supreme Court appointed Circuit Judge E. Richard Webber of Memphis, Missouri, to preside over the case. When JoAnn's attorney, Don Wolff, heard about the Webber appointment, he told a newspaper reporter, "I'm pleased about this. Webber is one of the top jurists in the state of Missouri. He's a man I admire and highly respect." Shortly before this, Webber had presided over the highly publicized murder trial of Ray and Faye Copeland, who were convicted of killing five transient workers and burying the bodies on their farm in northwestern Missouri. He imposed the death penalty on them.

■ ■ ■

In June of 1992, Webber denied two key motions which the defense attorneys had hoped to oust. One was to suppress the evidence related to the exhumation and autopsy of Sharon Williams's body. The other dealt with conflicts pertaining to the search warrant which did not state who tipped off the police about Walter's body being in the cistern. Without the bodies as evidence, the case had no basis. These two court rulings were a victory for the prosecution, and the case finally could proceed.

At the same time, Webber set the trial date for November 2, 1992. All the persistence exhibited by Kay and Walter Notheis paid off. Kay expressed relief when she heard about Webber's ruling. "My son disappeared almost nine years ago, and his body was found in the cistern over five years ago. I know we couldn't have gone on much longer. I just want to know why we have had to wait nine years?"

Jim's younger son, Brett, expressed similar sentiments about his mother's murder nine years before. "It's ruined my life. I want to see this settled so I can get on with it. I want to see that my mother's murder is rectified."

▪ ▪ ▪

During the five and a half years after finding Walter's body in Jim Williams's cistern, St. Charles County went through eight judges, two prosecuting attorneys, four assistant prosecutors, and over one hundred fifty motions filed by the defense.

Toward the middle of September, Dittmeier dug into the case. When the St. Charles County prosecutor's office finally delivered the boxes of files to Dittmeier's office at the Federal Building in St. Louis, he was appalled. Because he had to share the information with the defense, he called Don Wolff. Wolff remembered Dittmeier saying, "What a piece of shit this is! You ought to see these files."

Don responded, "I can imagine. If you want me to help get the thing organized, let's get together."

It took them over one hundred hours to go through the material and create order out of chaos.

Until the trial date, Dittmeier worked every day, fifteen hours a day, including weekends. He spent many days with Simcox and Uebinger. The three of them re-interviewed everyone who had previously given a statement.

All of Jim and JoAnn's neighbors in the Park Charles South subdivision had initially been tightlipped. But slowly, as the years passed, the closeness dissipated and some people felt Jim and JoAnn were guilty of murdering their former neighbor, Walter. Eventually, they told the police about their suspicions.

The Trans World Airlines personnel who knew Sharon Williams retold what they knew about Sharon and Jim, about his physically abusing her, about Sharon's strong suspicions that her husband was having an affair. Frank Floto, Jimi, Alice Almaroad, among a multitude of other people, were also interviewed again.

With the diligence and enthusiasm of both Simcox and Dittmeier, by November 2 the special prosecutor was ready to go to trial. Jim's trial would be heard first; JoAnn's, in February.

November 2, 1992–November 16, 1992. Nine years. It took this long before a trial ensued in the murders of Sharon Elaine Williams and Walter Simon Notheis, Jr. Nine years of anguish, tears, confusion, and bitterness for the families of these two victims. Nine years of denial from their accused murderers.

Before the actual trial could begin, a jury had to be selected. The court subpoenaed hundreds of people as prospective jurors. After one week of intense questioning by Dittmeier and Turken, twelve citizens qualified. On November 9, 1992, Judge Webber sequestered the jury, and day one of the trial began.

Dittmeier faced the juror's box and in his no-nonsense demeanor gave his opening statement for the State against James Howard Williams. For over an hour, without even one reference to his notes, he articulately described the inception of the affair between Jim and JoAnn. He explained how Jim wooed JoAnn with flowers and expensive gifts, and how the arguments between Jim and Sharon escalated as his affair intensified. Within months Jim inquired about a hit man to stage a murder to look like an accident. After one year into the affair, his wife died in a questionable accident, only later to be found through an autopsy that she was murdered.

Her murder was not enough. Although Jim could now freely see JoAnn, his lover still had to be cautious, especially when her husband came home. Dittmeier continued to tell the jurors that this major obstacle gnawed on Jim, that his obsession to want JoAnn completely for himself grew beyond rationality. A divorce would be the solution, but JoAnn told Jim that Walter refused to even consider this option. Jim told her not to worry. He had a plan.

The special prosecutor then explained Walter's demise, elaborating on the night and the following day that this renowned singer suddenly disappeared. Once Walter was no longer around, Jim began spending the nights at JoAnn's on December 28, the day she first reported her husband missing. Within a few weeks, he had moved his clothing and other personal belongings into his lover's house. Jim's dream materialized. JoAnn was his. Within two years, she divorced Walter and married Jim. And everything seemed to be fine. He loved JoAnn, he loved the twins, he loved the house. Then the autopsy on Sharon revealed she was murdered. After the police talked to Jim's sons about their mother's homicide, Jimi and Brett revealed information about the cistern. Once the police retrieved Walter's body, Jim's and JoAnn's idyllic world crashed.

When Dittmeier concluded his overview of the motivating factors leading to the murders, the judge asked Turken if he planned to make his opening statement. He declined until the State rested its case. Continuing, Dittmeier called six witnesses to testify for the State that first day. He began with Sharon's mother, Alice Almaroad. She gave her account of Sharon's death, of the funeral when Jim refused to attend the reception at her house, and of her grandson's new job at Hurley's Bar in Marion, including how Jimi could hitchhike anywhere. Dittmeier then called the deputy, firemen, and paramedics who were at the scene of Sharon's accident, most of whom had suspicions about her death.

His last witness of the day, Lynn Behrens, the ICU nurse at St. Joseph's Health Center, also gave details of Sharon's condition. She described the overwhelming gasoline odor on Sharon's body, and the burning on her own hands and arms when she bathed the accident victim. Although other personnel in the hospital expressed their doubts to each other about how Sharon died, as with the previous witnesses, no follow-up occurred at the time of her death.

▪ ▪ ▪

The next day, Chris Henson testified how Jim approached him looking for a hit man. When Mike Turken, Jim's defense attorney, cross-examined him as to why he didn't give this information to the law enforcement authorities until a few weeks before the trial, he said at first he and his fellow co-worker thought Jim was joking. Yet after Sharon's death, they called one another and talked about Jim's request. But because neither wanted to get involved, they only spoke about it with each other and their respective families.

Jim's son, Brett, also gave his testimony on November 10 as a prosecution witness. He knew about his father's affair with JoAnn. And he knew his parents' arguments increased dramatically during this period. Some people outside of the family also knew that during these outbursts, Jim would grab Sharon by her shoulders and shake her violently. Of the two sons, Brett idolized his father. But to think his father caused his mother's death, turned the hero love to hate. Brett continued to relate various incidents about the day of his mother's funeral and his father's paramount obsession for JoAnn.

The last witness that second day was the evasive Bruce Schone. Almost everyone felt he knew what happened the night of Walter's disappearance, but he refused to cooperate and reveal any details. As Turken cross-examined Schone about Walter coming into his garage the afternoon of December 27, he asked if they had discussed the sale of any drugs. Immediately, Dittmeier objected.

During the side-bar, this is when lawyers privately discuss issues of the case with the judge, Dittmeier told Webber, "I object to this whole line of questioning. It's immaterial and irrelevant. And under the law it appears that they are trying to set up some sort of a sham defendant here, which, there is no evidence that anybody else committed this murder."

Turken responded, "I think there is going to be evidence that there may have been another motive to kill him."

The judge overruled Dittmeier's objection.

But when Turken proceeded with the question about a drug sale, Schone said he and Walter did not discuss one.

Once more in this trial, Jim's older son, Jimi, was mentioned. As Turken cross-examined Schone, he asked about "Bigfoot," one of Jimi's nicknames because when he broke into people's apartments or houses, he would kick the door in with his size fifteen foot. Schone had known Jimi from dealing drugs in his short-lived venture of being a bar owner. Turken tried to infer that Jimi might also have known Walter through Schone; thus, some conspiracy could have been planned.

As Turken continued questioning Schone, he asked if Schone's wife called him at the garage the night Walter disappeared. He said he didn't remember. When the questioning focused on Detective Rich Fagen and Deputy Ray Runyon offering Schone immunity, Dittmeier again objected and asked for another side-bar.

"Judge, for the record, after the body was found, the police continued to investigate this guy, because they felt somebody had driven a car, perhaps for Mr. Williams, and they felt that Schone had evidence about the murder. This witness was asked if he would take a polygraph test and talk to a lawyer. He said that he didn't want to, and that he wasn't going to make any more statements."

Turken emphasized that he would not inquire about the polygraph. Again, Dittmeier didn't see how this was relevant to the case. But Turken reiterated that Schone refused to cooperate with the investigation and that everyone assumed he was the last person who could have seen Walter.

Turken's adamant stand continued. "This witness was offered immunity, refuses to cooperate, refuses to testify, and I think that's relevant to his credibility as a witness on the stand here."

Judge Webber told Jim's defense attorney that he may show bias and prejudice, but he was not to attempt getting into any polygraph. Turken assured him he wouldn't, and cross-examination resumed.

"Were you offered immunity from prosecution, sir?"

Schone glanced at Dittmeier. "Should I answer?"

Dittmeier told him he should.

"Yeah," said Schone, "in a roundabout way."

"Did you not corroborate until after you were offered immunity?"

"I cooperated with them. Are you talking about the incident when him and..."

"Hold on," commanded Turken. Turning to Webber, he said, "Judge, I'm concerned. I don't want to get into the areas the Court has indicated we shouldn't get into."

Dittmeier interjected and thought Schone should be allowed to respond. But Judge Webber felt differently and ordered a recess.

At the side-bar the judge explained that either of the attorneys could inform Schone that he did not have to volunteer to the open court that he took a polygraph test. Dittmeier responded, "But he didn't take one, Judge."

"Right. He didn't take one, and I think one may have been requested," said Turken. "But, boy, gosh, yeah, I don't want him to all of a sudden blurt something out and scare the hell out of me, too."

"I won't ask for a mistrial if he does," stated Dittmeier.

"I understand you won't, but I don't know what I'll do. Yeah, I understand the Court's concern, it's mine also," said Turken.

Turning the microphone back on, Judge Webber said, "Court will again be in session."

Webber looked at Turken, "You may proceed."

"I think I have ended my examination, Your Honor."

Then Webber turned to Dittmeier. "Redirect?"

"No, I have no further questions."

In less than a minute after court resumed, Schone walked off the stand. This key witness, who could have been far more extensively cross-examined and perhaps could have told the court what had happened to Walter Scott on December 27, 1983, left the courtroom. Many people listening to Schone's testimony expressed shock and felt that a deal had been cut with him, and that the public would not be privy to this information. The second day of the trial ended.

▪ ▪ ▪

Day three of the trial proved to be busy as eight witnesses testified for the State. Scott Henderson, who used to be good friends with JoAnn and Walter, took the stand. He stated that JoAnn had called him and his wife around one-thirty or two on the morning of December 28 saying she was worried about Walter. During the conversation she said Walter had gone to get a battery from Bruce Schone's garage, but a couple of hours later Schone told her Walter never arrived.

Henderson also stated that JoAnn told him she knew Walter had gone downtown to the Mansion House Center. When Henderson asked her how she knew that, she said she had contacted Jim Williams on his mobile phone and told him that Walter would soon leave the house. She also told Henderson that later in the evening Jim contacted her and said he had followed Walter down to the Mansion House Center and saw him pull into the parking area. Jim then returned to St. Charles. In none of the police statements had JoAnn offered this information.

The testimony from witnesses centered on the last day anyone had seen or talked to Walter, and the few days following his disappearance, especially Jim's remarks to Linn Wise about Walter being "long gone," and Ed Eckert's testimony about Jim and JoAnn's trip to Pennsylvania and discovering the sexually explicit pictures, along with the sex gadgets in Walter's trailer.

Both of Walter's parents told about conversations with their son during his visit home. They also elaborated on the last time they had seen Walter and his family on Christmas day, and gave an account about the three days after their son's disappearance.

When Turken cross-examined Walter, Sr., he asked him if his son had been having any problems.

Walter wryly responded, "Yeah, I imagine he did. He got killed, didn't he."

Upon Turken's cross-examination of Kay Notheis, she described how Jim stayed at her son's house most of the day and evening when she and her husband were there on December 28. "He was there all the time, never gone but only a half an hour at a time."

Turken stated, "He was fairly open about being there. I mean, it's hard to hide him, isn't it?"

"Yeah, nervy."

Turken tried to rephrase her response. "Open, correct?"

"He lived there; he should have been."

After court recessed for the day, Kay told a reporter who kidded her about being argumentative with Turken, "I've waited too long to let him twist my words."

▪ ▪ ▪

The next day, November 12, the last two witnesses for the State testified: Gretchen Brown, a friend and co-worker of Sharon's; and Dr. Mary Case, the Chief Medical Examiner.

Brown told the court about her visit to Jim's house after Sharon's death and how Jim told her he was in love with JoAnn. She also said that Jim told her Walter was abusive to his family, involved in drugs and gambling, and that one day something was going to happen to him. Jim proceeded to take Brown upstairs and showed her a closet full of clothes he had bought JoAnn for Christmas.

Dittmeier then asked Brown if she had ever received a call from Jim when she was at work as a TWA reservationist.

"Yes, he wanted me to check the flight schedules from some town in Pennsylvania and see if the flights were coming in at the time he thought Walter Scott would be arriving."

When Turken cross-examined Brown, he asked, "Didn't Jim also say that Walter was affiliated with the Mafia?"

"Yes."

"Wasn't it at that point that Jim says that something is going to happen to Walter?"

"Yes."

After having her restate that Jim told her that Walter was supposed to have been an abusive father and husband, a heavy gambler, involved with drugs, alcohol, and the Mafia, Turken had no further questions.

In his redirect examination, Dittmeier asked, "Did he ever tell you that he knew Walter Scott personally?"

"No."

"So, you don't know if he was getting that from JoAnn, or you don't know where he was getting that information, is that correct?"

"Right."

"And, as you sit here today, is it your testimony that he told you that something was going to happen to Walter Scott some day?"

"Yes."

"I have no further questions."

While Case proceeded to give her testimony about her findings regarding Sharon Williams's autopsy and display graphic pictures to the jury, several people in the courtroom said Jim would not look at Case or the pictures. Instead, they said that he stared down at the table.

As Dittmeier attempted to question Case if the injuries which Sharon had sustained were consistent with the traffic accident, Turken's associate, Ellsworth Cundiff, Jr., who conducted the cross-examination of Case's testimony, kept objecting. And Judge Webber kept overruling.

Finally, Case stated, "The nature and magnitude of these injuries, in my opinion, are inconsistent with the accident in which Sharon Williams was said to have sustained these injuries."

In Cundiff's cross-examination, he tried to infer that the three attending physicians at the hospital and a forensic odontologist, Dr. Homer Campbell, with Forensic Consultants, Inc., in New Mexico, Missouri, all disagreed with Case's opinion that Sharon's death resulted from two linear blows to the back of her head.

When Dittmeier did his redirect, he guided his questions toward Case to indicate that the hospital physicians were only told their patient had been involved in an auto accident; they were unaware of it being minor in nature.

To further clarify Dr. Campbell's qualifications, Dittmeier asked Case about Campbell's area of expertise.

"He's a dentist," said Case. "He's neither a neuropathologist nor a forensic pathologist. He's not a physician. He's a dentist."

"Despite his not agreeing with your opinion that the victim's death resulted from two linear blows to the back of the head, didn't he agree with your opinion that this could not have been caused in a traffic accident?"

"Yes, he agreed with that part of my opinion."

"And those attending physicians at the hospital are not forensic pathologists, are they?"

"No, they are not."

"Those physicians' primary goal is not to determine whether it's an accident or a homicide?"

Cundiff interjected, "Your Honor, I'm going to object as to leading the witness."

"Sustained."

Dittmeier rephrased the question. "Do you know of anything, when those physicians are treating a patient like this, that would cause them to determine the manner of death?"

"No, that's not at all the function of an attending physician. And, in fact, they are not allowed to sign death certificates unless they are a natural manner of death."

As Cundiff recrossed he tried to show that Case was a well-known expert witness in forensic pathology who often testified for the State. "Ma'am, how many times have you testified in cases where death was involved?"

"Many times. Several hundred."

"And have you always testified for the State?"

"Because of the nature of my job, I provide testimony for whoever calls me. But usually in a criminal case, with a few exceptions, I've been called by the prosecution."

As Dittmeier came back for further redirect, he wanted to emphasize his point about Sharon's death. "And in this case you have made a determination that this is not an accident, is that right?"

"This is not an accident."

"And do you know of anything in that Cadillac automobile that could have caused those two separate blows to the back of the head?"

"No, I do not."

"I have no further questions."

"Recross?" asked Judge Webber.

Cundiff replied, "I have nothing further."

Because Case was his last witness, Dittmeier said, "The State is prepared to rest, Your Honor."

After the judge dismissed the jury for the day, Turken gave him a Defendant's Motion to Dismiss at the Close of the State's Evidence. He also had two to three pages of points that he felt the Court improperly allowed and admitted as evidence over objection. The next day Turken would begin with the defense witnesses.

■ ■ ■

At nine o'clock in the morning, the attorneys met in Judge Webber's chambers for further proceedings. For half an hour they discussed various technicalities about the case. One of the first issues dealt with Dittmeier just filing a Motion in Limine. In effect, it stated that just because other people might have had a motive to commit a crime, unless there would be direct evidence linking them to the case, any reference to this would be inadmissible.

Turken argued there was already evidence in the case that others may have been involved. He said there were certain statements made by witnesses that dealt directly with other individuals' complicity.

Judge Webber said, "The only evidence has been suggestion that there were telephone calls, and various people said he was into drugs and the Mafia, but no specific individuals that I can recall."

"I think Mr. Schone was identified as having involvement."

"In what respect?" asked the judge.

"I think that the evidence is going to show that Schone was involved, and I have to be able to present that evidence that he was involved in the death. I don't see how I can be prohibited from doing it."

"Well, okay, if you can show direct involvement, then it is true, you would be able to adduce the evidence. But there will have to be some direct evidence cited."

After going over further details, they entered the courtroom and the day's proceedings began with Turken's opening statement. He informed the jury that the defendant didn't have to present any evidence in the case, but would. The first thing Turken told the twelve jurors was that Jim was not guilty for either offense. Since these were two cases, not one, he instructed them to look at the evidence for each one separately. Further, he emphasized that the State gave no evidence indicating that Jim was responsible for Sharon's death. Turken added that the police department and law officials failed to investigate the offenses thoroughly. And just because they knew about Jim and JoAnn's affair, they put on blinders and assumed the accused were guilty.

Toward the end of his opening statement, Turken said they would be hearing evidence about how the singer who made the song "The Cheater" a national hit record was, in actuality, the cheater. Jim and JoAnn had told the police about finding drugs in Walter's car and the threatening phone calls Walter received, but the police didn't investigate this. He finished his statement by telling the jury that Jim Williams had not been proven guilty. And that once they considered all the evidence, they would serve justice by acquitting him.

Turken called the first defense witness, William Lawson, to the stand that Friday, November 13, 1992. He lived close to the site of Sharon's accident. On that particular night he remembered seeing a blond-haired woman driving a new yellow Cadillac past his trailer. A minute or so later, a dark-haired lady followed. Shortly after this, Lawson heard sirens.

Twenty minutes later as the ambulance passed by his trailer with its siren shrieking into the night air, he said he saw the woman with the blond hair in it. Then he saw the tow truck pass, hauling the Cadillac behind it. Lawson told the court the car had sustained a lot of damage.

His statement contradicted numerous people at the scene. One of the paramedics testified that while he treated Sharon in the car, he took off her blond wig and threw it in the back seat. In addition, everyone at the scene and afterwards said the car's damage was minimal.

Another defense witness, Ed Litteken, one of the firemen at the scene, said he smelled gasoline when he got to the car, yet he didn't recall any odor while transporting Sharon in the ambulance. This was another contradictory statement contrasting other emergency personnel in the ambulance and at the hospital.

Turken brought Schone back into the forefront when he asked his fourth witness, Norm Forgue, the policeman who taped a conversation with JoAnn at his house, "Did she say to you, 'Bruce Schone knows what happened to my husband'?"

Forgue answered, "She made reference to that, yes, sir."

Turken's next defense witness, Ray Runyon, who in 1992 was the Sheriff of St. Charles County, indicated that he had known the defendant for twenty years. After Sharon's death, he had gone to the lot where her car was impounded, and noticed very little body damage. Although he didn't tell the court that day, he had told other people that it puzzled him about how Sharon could have died as a result of such a minor accident. And as with previous witnesses, Turken again mentioned Schone. The defense attorney stressed Schone's reluctance to speak about Walter's murder and his refusal to cooperate with the authorities.

The last witness of the day was Scott Peterson, the realtor who listed Jim's home. He stated that when he inspected the property to record its description, that Jim showed him around the back yard. Peterson said he was completely unaware of the cistern until Jim pointed to the flower planter and told him there was one under it. If Jim had not mentioned it, very few people would have known it existed. Peterson stressed that the defendant gave him this information voluntarily.

■ ■ ■

The trial continued for a few hours on Saturday morning, November 14, 1992. The youngest son of Walter Notheis, Jr., Bryan, now twenty years old, testified for Jim Williams's defense, his father's accused murderer.

During the first part of his testimony, he told of an unrelated incident when one night his father came running into the house, waving both of his handguns in the air and shouting for Bryan and his cousin to get on the floor. He gave no explanation as to why his father felt his life was endangered. Bryan also told about his father receiving harassing phone calls from a man with a gruff voice. His testimony inferred that his father's murder could have been mob-related.

Further attestation centered on Walter's visits to Bruce Schone's garage. Even though Bryan indicated his father didn't need any auto work done on his vehicles, he said he and his father visited the garage four or five times over his last time home. On a few of the visits he took his black bag into the garage with him. Bryan said one of his dad's guns was in the bag; the other, under the seat of the Suburban. When Turken asked what else Bryan had seen in the bag over the years, Walter's son told him, "Money and pills."

Then he related the events on the night of his father's disappearance. He said after his father had been gone a couple of hours, Schone called the house inquiring about Walter's whereabouts, since he had never shown up at the garage. His mother, he continued, appeared visibly concerned. Shortly thereafter, Bryan kissed his mother good night and went to bed. When he awoke that Wednesday morning at seven-thirty and went downstairs, he saw Deputy A. C. Blanks at the kitchen table taking information for a Missing Person's Report.

After the officer left, Bryan said he suggested that Jim and his mother look in his father's briefcase for any information. They did. When everyone wondered where Walter could be, Bryan suggested looking for his father's car at the airport. They did. When the two band members returned his father's Suburban from Pennsylvania, Bryan found the bag of one hundred fifty orange and yellow pills under its dash.

Bryan also admitted to snooping around his father's personal belongings prior to December 27 and finding several letters from

Serina. He said he showed his mother the letters. It was at this point she told her eleven year old twins that she intended getting a divorce after the holidays.

As he continued his testimony, Bryan told the court that on the night of December 28, 1983, he was scared and asked Jim to spend the night. He also added he didn't recall the Lincoln Town car having any problems.

When Dittmeier cross-examined Bryan, he began, "You had just turned eleven years old in August of that year, had you not?"

"That's correct."

"If I understand this correctly, you were eleven years old when they brought the Suburban back. And even though your mother and Jim Williams had gone through the Suburban up in Pennsylvania, you are the one that searched it and found the pills, right?"

"That's correct."

"And you were eleven years old," continued the prosecutor, emphasizing the word eleven, "and you were the one that thought to go to the airport to find the car, isn't that right?"

"Amongst other places, yes."

"And you were eleven years old and were the one that thought that they should go upstairs and get the briefcase to find out about your dad's whereabouts, right?"

"Right."

Dittmeier paused and raised an eyebrow. He then asked Bryan about the pornographic magazines that his mother had found when she searched Walter's personal belongings in Pennsylvania and why she gave them to the police when she knew Walter had several of those magazines hidden throughout the house.

"Because she found vibrators with them, I guess. And other sex toys."

"Your mother turned over to the police on January 3, 1984, the .22-caliber revolver, the .25-caliber revolver, boxes of pornography, a briefcase, and an unknown quantity of Darvon and Valium, right?"

"That's correct."

"Okay, going back to the briefcase. Were the efforts of examining the jewelry in your father's briefcase designed to find your father some way?"

"I don't think the jewelry had any clues to where my dad had disappeared. But looking through his belongings, yes, that could have given us clues."

"So," continued Dittmeier, "looking at the jewelry and deciding what was good and bad was just something to do to kill the time?"

"No."

"I mean, wasn't the focus on your father's whereabouts unknown?"

"It was in relation because my dad didn't wear his real jewelry. He had all these new rings, and we had no money."

"So, at that point the issue wasn't finding your father. It was determining whether it was good jewelry or bad jewelry, is that right?"

"We had no money."

After a few more questions, Bryan Notheis was excused.

Turken called Joseph Peters as his next witness. Peters had known Walter since they were both teenagers. He told Turken during the last six months of Walter's life that Walter had been very nervous, uptight, scared. Yet when Dittmeier cross-examined him, he admitted that the last year of Walter's life he had only seen him a couple of times.

Everyone close to Walter knew that since his early twenties he carried a gun, never positioned his back to anyone, scrutinized a place thoroughly before entering it, and had been generally overly cautious. The testimony Peters gave did not indicate any new personality behavior that last year of Walter's life.

At ten forty-seven, Judge Webber told the attorneys at his bench, "This concludes the festivities for today. I'll excuse the jury and explain that court will be in recess until nine o'clock on Monday."

Turning on his microphone, he stated, "Ladies and gentlemen, please remain seated and silent while the jury exits."

▪ ▪ ▪

On November 16, 1992, James Howard Williams, Sr., took the stand. His three hundred fifty pound frame filled the witness chair. After Turken directed his client through the night of Sharon's accident and the days following her death, he focused on the relationship between Jim and JoAnn.

"You didn't make any effort to conceal the fact that you and JoAnn were friends, is that right?"

"No, I did not."

"At some point in time in early December, did she tell you she was planning on getting a divorce?"

"Yes, she said she planned on it after the holidays."

"And, did she tell you that she'd told the kids that?"

"Yes."

In respect to Gretchen Brown's visit at his house after Sharon's death, he said she arrived around six-thirty and left around ten that evening. During this time, he fixed her car and then he prepared dinner for the two of them. As they ate, they reminisced about Sharon. Later, Jim said, he showed Gretchen some clothes in the bedroom closet, which he indicated he had bought for Sharon's birthday, not for JoAnn's Christmas presents.

Regarding the afternoon of December 27, 1983, he stated he had just arrived at Hackmann's Lumber when JoAnn called him on his mobile phone. During the course of the conversation, she told him that Walter went to Schone's garage for a car inspection. Jim left and drove to Ken's Auto Supply, across from the garage, to purchase a few things. He informed the court that when he was at Ken's, he saw Walter talking to a big man in an overcoat, wearing a black rimmed hat. This unknown individual got into his luxury car and took off, as did Walter. From the auto supply store, Jim told Turken that he stopped by

Pizza Hut, then a convenience store to get cigaretttes before going home. He never mentioned following Walter down to the Mansion House.

He continued with his testimony that JoAnn had called him a few times that evening expressing concern that Walter had not shown up at Schone's garage. At four or five the next morning, he said she woke him up with another call telling him Walter still had not come home and that she was upset. That's when he told her he would call his deputy friend, Ray Runyon.

After going through the next few days' events, Turken asked when he had moved into JoAnn's. Jim told him the last part of March, the first of April. He emphasized he did not sleep with JoAnn, that Bryan and Mindy slept with her.

As Turken guided Jim's testimony to the incident of constructing the flower planter on top of the cistern, Jim said, "I was going to build a wishing well on there for Sharon, and...never got it done."

He also stated that since he was having a new deck built, he thought it would be a good idea to also have a flower planter cover the cistern. When Turken asked him why he had told the realtor about the cistern being there, Jim stated, "I didn't want to sell the property, have it cave in and somebody fall in there and me be liable for it. I wanted to make sure that he knew there was a brick-lined cistern that could collapse."

▪ ▪ ▪

During cross-examination, Dittmeier questioned Jim about statements he made that he and JoAnn were just friends. "Now, you had told your son, Brett, that you wanted to make a life with JoAnn and her family?"

Jim quietly responded, "If someday that was possible, yes."

"But she was just a friend at that point, right?"

"Yes."

"But you already made up your mind that you wanted to make a life with this friend and her family?"

"I can't say I made up my mind, no. I told Brett that I thought a lot of her, but I never told him I loved her."

"Okay," continued Dittmeier. "And you didn't tell Gretchen Brown you loved JoAnn either?"

"No."

"So, they both got that confused, I assume?"

"I would think so, yes."

"So, you wanted to make a life with somebody that you didn't love?"

"Well, I figured if we could work some things out later, why we would eventually fall in love, maybe."

When Dittmeier questioned Jim about telling the two neighbors, Wise and Callabrese, on the way over to pick up Walter's car at the airport that Walter was 'long gone,' Jim said, "I didn't say that. I told them that he probably flew the coop and went somewhere else."

Dittmeier began grilling Jim. "So, you weren't concerned at all at finding him in that car, were you?"

"Yes, I was concerned. I wanted to find him and get him back."

"Why did you want to find him to get him back?"

"Well, I was just as concerned as anybody else."

Dittmeier raised his eyebrows. "You thought a lot of the guy?"

"No, I didn't, I mean, I didn't even really know the guy, but I didn't want to see his whole family tore up."

Then Dittmeier changed his tactic. "Did you know he carried a gun?"

"Yeah, from what people told me."

"And you were over there sleeping on his couch all night, is that right?"

Jim nodded. "That's correct."

"In his home?"

"Yes."

"But you didn't know he was dead and he could have walked right in on you, isn't that correct?"

"That's correct."

"Weren't you concerned?" asked Dittmeier.

"I was concerned to the point where if he walked in, I would have faced that bridge when I came to it," responded Jim.

After Dittmeier cross-examined Jim, Turken had a few more questions, then he announced that the defense rested.

■ ■ ■

Turken's closing emphasized that the whole case was based on circumstantial evidence, that there was no direct evidence of his client's guilt. "With all the detectives and the forensic labs and DNA tests, where is the proof in fingerprints that Mr. Williams drove Walter Scott's car? Where are the lab tests on the pills found in Mr. Scott's Suburban? What about the yellow rope used to bound Mr. Scott? My associate, Mr. Cundiff, bought several feet of it at Central Hardware over the noon hour. It's identical to the kind Mr. Williams had in his garage."

Turken keenly looked at the jurors. "This is guilt? The State hasn't proven anything. Everything is based on circumstantial evidence."

Again, he mentioned Bruce Schone. He described Schone's body language during his testimony, that this uncooperative key figure in the case kept looking down at his shoes. That he always averted his eyes, never looking directly at anyone. Turken also mentioned that Mark Lee, the assistant St. Charles prosecuting attorney, had offered Schone immunity, inferring that perhaps a deal had been cut.

Another person Turken targeted as a possible suspect was Jimi, Jr. He stated that Jimi had a motive to frame his father for his mother's murder. Because even Jimi's grandmother had told the Court that Jimi could hitchhike anywhere, it would be nothing for Jimi to hitchhike from Marion to St. Louis the night of December 27. And, Turken stressed it was Jimi who told the police about the cistern.

▪ ▪ ▪

During Dittmeier's closing statement, he reiterated the main points of the case against Jim. Then he focused on the innuendoes. "During the whole thing, Mr. Turken is trying to lay the scenario about the Mafia: New Orleans Mafia, New York Mafia. Do you think the Mafia sent a hit man down here and they hit Walter Notheis, and then not knowing what else to do, they rode through St. Charles County and happened to pull up to 5647 Gutermuth, where just by chance JoAnn Notheis's boyfriend lived? And they happened to look around and saw a cistern there? Then they got out and with a bar pried the top off the cistern and threw Mr. Scott's body into the water while Mr. Williams is home all night? Ladies and gentlemen, that's ridiculous.

"Then there's Jimi, Jr. Granted, he may not be the finest person in the world, having been in the penitentiary much of his adult life. But think about what Mr. Williams is doing when he starts pointing the finger at his own son to save himself. I think that gives you a little bit of an idea of what kind of character we have here."

Dittmeier also stated that JoAnn tried to manipulate the legal system when she told Turken that the police didn't investigate Schone. When Turken objected, Dittmeier's closing was interrupted and they had a side-bar. Before the trial began, Dittmeier gave Turken proof that Schone had been thoroughly investigated. Now at the judge's bench he asked the defense attorney, "Did JoAnn lie to you?" Turken quietly replied, "Yes."

Continuing, Dittmeier told the court that Jim also manipulated Ray Runyon in the early morning hours of December 28 when he told Runyon, "JoAnn's distraught and I've been over here most of the night. How do I make a police report?"

Dittmeier said Jim was, in effect, laying the ground work for an alibi.

In his low-keyed manner, the special prosecutor said, "Jim's gentle, kind, and friendly," he paused for several seconds, "until someone gets in the way of what he wants. And what he wanted was JoAnn. Two cold-blooded murders were committed by a greedy individual who was and still is obsessed by JoAnn Notheis."

Looking at each jury member, he said, "I hope you will use your common sense and come back with a guilty verdict on both counts."

▪ ▪ ▪

The jury left to deliberate at six-twenty in the evening. At eleven o'clock that night, they returned with their verdict.

In his stately black gown, Judge Webber walked into the courtroom from his chambers and sat down. Jim stood next to his attorney, took a deep breath and visibly let it out. Turken leaned toward his client and inaudibly whispered. Jim stood straighter. Everyone in the courtroom became silent.

After glancing at some papers, Webber looked up and stared at the jurors. "Ladies and gentlemen of the jury, and each of you, have you arrived at your verdict?"

Juror Stevens responded, "Yes, we have, Your Honor." He handed a piece of paper to the bailiff, who in turn handed it to the judge. Unfolding the paper, he read aloud, "As to Count I, regarding the death of Sharon Elaine Williams, we, the jury, find the defendant, James Howard Williams, Sr., guilty of capital murder. Is that your verdict?"

Collectively, all twelve jurors said, "Yes."

The quiet erupted into cheers and sighs of relief for the people wanting retribution for Walter's and Sharon's murders, while Jim's supporters gasped and protested loudly in disbelief.

After Judge Webber quieted the outcry, he continued reading, "As to Count II, regarding the death of Walter Simon Notheis, Jr., we the jury, find the defendant, James Howard Williams, Sr., guilty of capital murder. Is that your verdict?"

Again, a collective "yes."

Pandemonium once more exploded across the room. People clung to each other, either from joy or from anguish. Tears streaked many faces for the same opposing reasons. Jim's shoulders slumped and his head bowed in defeat as he stood crying next to his defense attorney. Turken patted him on his large shoulders, trying to reassure Jim that he would appeal the verdicts immediately.

After the courtroom cleared, the judge allowed an unusual incident to occur, which left many people aghast. He told Jim he could spend his last night at home with JoAnn. The next day the jurors would decide Jim's sentence: either life in prison or death by lethal injection.

November 17, 1992–January 11, 1993. The next morning after spending two hours going over various documents in the judge's chambers, court resumed at twelve-twenty for the penalty hearing. Somber faces and an occasional whisper replaced the frenetic outburst from the previous night. Jim didn't give his supporters a big smile or a friendly nod today. His normal cheerfulness seemed to have crumpled to dust, and an aura of defeat wrapped around his massive bulk.

Before the jury would decide Jim's fate of life imprisonment or death, Judge Webber allowed nine character witnesses to take the stand and plead for Jim's life. Becky Barrett, a former neighbor of Jim and Sharon's, had known Jim for over twenty-five years. She told the jurors that Jim was like a big brother to her and that her children called him "Uncle Jim." Besides Jim always being available to talk about personal problems, Barrett added that if she ever needed something fixed around the house, he would be right over and take care of it. "That's just the way he was," she said.

Sharon Metz also stated how Jim had been kind to her children. They called him "Mr. Jim." When her daughter was three or four, she had been afraid of storms. "One time," Metz related, "he reached into a deep pocket in his bib overalls and pulled out an iron bolt. 'Here,' he said to her daughter, placing it in her small hand. 'Take this. From now on, this will be your good luck charm. Anytime a storm comes up, just pull it out and hold onto it. You'll see, you won't be afraid again.'"

Not only did Jim help Metz's daughter overcome her fear of storms, but she said he also stayed up many nights talking to her and her husband about their son, a recovering drug addict. Because of Jimi's association with drugs, Jim felt he could commiserate with them and offer some advice.

Another witness, Jim Steiner, had known Jim for nine years. Although he was a firefighter with the St. Louis Fire Department, on his days off Steiner worked for Jim, doing odd jobs to earn extra money. He told the jury, "One of the things that I always felt good about when I worked for Jim was he always had patience. He'd say, 'If you got a problem, we can work it out and get it done.' He was always there when you needed him."

As the witnesses praised Jim in the courtroom, he tried to fight back his tears, but soon they flowed down to his thick mustache. After giving their testimony, his friends walked over to him to pat his back or give him a quick hug. Several times Jim took off his wire-rimmed glasses to wipe his weary looking eyes with a handkerchief.

After the character testimony, Dittmeier approached the jury box. In his unwavering manner, he told the jurors, "You have now reached the point where you are going to have to assess the punishment in this case after listening to all the evidence. And the punishment will either be a death sentence or a life sentence. It's a big decision.

"You've heard about Sharon Williams's murder. A wantonly vile and inhumane death to be bludgeoned in the head and doused with gasoline. That's depravity of mind, ladies and gentlemen.

You also heard about the death of Walter Notheis, of how he was bound, shot in the back, and stuffed into a well for over three years. You saw the grisly pictures of both victims. I won't wave them in front of you again. But once more, we're talking about another wantonly vile and inhumane death. Both were innocent victims. Both were helpless.

"Just a short time ago you heard about one woman saying Jim was an ideal husband. Yet here he was giving gifts to JoAnn, wanting JoAnn, but married to Sharon. That's not what most people would consider an ideal husband. You heard another woman tell you how Jim counseled them when her son was involved with drugs." Dittmeier turned toward Jim. "What about his own son, Jimi? He got released from the penitentiary on Christmas day. Who had to pick him up? His grandmother, Alice Almaroad. Where was Jim? Why didn't he counsel his own son?

"The people you heard today cried legitimate tears, they weren't put-on. Yet how many tears has Alice Almaroad, Sharon's mother, shed? Or, how many tears have Walter and Kay Notheis shed? And what about the children of these two victims? Two lost their mother; four lost their father. What about them?

"Jim has been described as a very gregarious, outgoing guy who's nice to everybody," Dittmeier briefly paused, "unless they are in his way and he's not getting what he wants. And that murder of Sharon Williams turned on two things: greed and lust. Greed, because he didn't want to lose the business. This man sitting here tells his son, Brett, 'I can't afford to divorce your mother because I've worked hard for the business, and she'll rake me over the coals and get it all.' But he wasn't going to give JoAnn up either. Nobody was there to appeal for Sharon Williams's life.

"Then he went from his wife's murder to stalking Walter Notheis. Granted, during the course of this trial, you haven't heard a lot of good things about Walter Scott, but don't you think if somebody stringed people in here, they would say he was a wonderful friend, a wonderful entertainer?

"But that's not what you are here for today. You are here to assess the punishment for Jim Williams, for his two cold-blooded, calculated murders. Think back to his testimony. Did he ever tell you, 'I didn't kill my wife.' Did you notice that? He never said it. And he never said 'I didn't kill Walter Notheis.' For two hours he testified, and not once did he say this; not once did he show remorse."

Looking at each member of the jury, Dittmeier concluded his appeal. "You've heard the evidence. You know how cold-blooded these murders were. On behalf of Alice Almaroad, Kay and Walter Notheis, I'm asking you to come back and assess his punishment at death."

After Dittmeier sat down, Mike Turken stood up and slowly approached the jurors. "Your concerns at this point are to appropriately punish Mr. Williams, and, I guess, to protect the community. That's your job as the jury. And you can accomplish both without having to kill Jim Williams.

"The judge has instructed you to consider the mitigating evidence. Those things you have to consider are Jim's prior history; his physical condition; the fact he had military service; and the people who have come in to testify. You have to consider all of these things.

"As you know, it takes all twelve of you to agree to Mr. Williams's punishment. I hope one of you stands up for your conscience, for your feelings, and realize that this is not a case with which to impose the death sentence. You should tell yourself that the State has not proven any one of those aggravating circumstances beyond a reasonable doubt."

He walked closer to the jurors, took off his glasses, and looked at them intently. "You can extend mercy to Jim, and only you can. That's your decision. I stand before you and ask you to show mercy to Jim Williams. In a civilized society, we don't take an eye for an eye. To do that, would be torture, would be barbarian.

"Don't confuse life without the possibility of probation or parole for fifty years with the old life sentence. That's the one that used to mean that you could get out." Turken pointed toward Jim. "He'll never be set free. He'll die in prison. Killing Jim Williams will not accomplish anything. It won't bring back Sharon. It won't bring back Mr. Scott. We can't undo what has already been done. Mr. Williams will be punished for the rest of his life if you elect life in prison."

Quietly scanning each juror's face, Turken ended his statement. "Sentence Jim Williams to life without the possibility of parole. Thank you."

▪ ▪ ▪

Two hours later the jurors came back with their verdict. Jim stood up, took a deep breath and shook his head slightly. Pressing his lips tightly together, he listened as Judge Webber told him, "We, the jury, having found the defendant guilty on Counts I and II in the deaths of Sharon Elaine Williams and Walter Simon Notheis, Jr., respectively, fix the punishment of imprisonment for life without eligibility for probation or parole."

As a deputy handcuffed Jim and led him out of the courtroom, several of Jim's friends cried and yelled out, "We love you, Jim."

Outside the courtroom, Wally Notheis, Walter's oldest son, expressed disappointment. "Jim Williams's family can visit him in prison. How often can I see my dad?"

When he walked out of the courthouse, Mike Turken told reporters, "I'm going to seek a new trial. I don't think the last chapter has been written in this book."

■ ■ ■

Although the jury imposed their sentence on Jim, Judge Webber also had to administer his. On January 12, 1993, Jim walked back into the courtroom in his bright orange jail-issue suit. Judge E. Richard Webber read his sentence. He concurred with the jury. The rest of Jim's life would be spent locked away from society, from his friends and family.

Now that Jim's trial was over, JoAnn awaited her fate.

December, 1992–April 27, 1993. Jim's future had been determined by the twelve jurors in November. JoAnn now faced hers. None of the evidence against Jim in his trial would be admissible in hers. Tom Dittmeier knew he had a problem.

During the first part of December, Dittmeier called JoAnn's attorney, Don Wolff. "Don, is there any way we can dispose of this case."

Don replied, "Not if you plan it being heard on charges of murder or even conspiracy to commit murder. I know you're in a tight place, Tom. You don't have any evidence on JoAnn."

"There are a few things, but maybe not enough for a conviction. I know she had made some false statements. Let me do some research on this and get back with you."

■ ■ ■

Several days later Dittmeier again called St. Louis's well known defense attorney. "Don, I found out that a false statement is a misdemeanor, and no way in hell I'll agree to a slap on the wrist. But while checking on this, I looked into concealment. When she made some statements to the police which were false and didn't reveal them, she was, in fact, concealing this information."

"What would the charge be?"

"Hindering the prosecution. A felony. She could get up to five years."

"You'd drop the first-degree murder charge?" asked Wolff.

"I'd consider it."

"What did she conceal?"

"You know as well as I do, Don. She didn't tell the cops that she called Jim to tell him that Walter was getting ready to leave for Schone's, and that Jim supposedly followed him downtown to the Mansion House."

"Yeah, okay."

"Do you think JoAnn would go for it?"

"I don't know. Let me talk to her. I'll get back with you."

▪ ▪ ▪

When Wolff first met JoAnn, he said he found her very vulnerable and sad. She came across as having a hard edge about her, but he perceived that was only an outer facade to protect herself from getting emotionally hurt.

He stated, "Walter Scott had fame and popularity, whereas JoAnn stayed in St. Louis raising their two children and taking care of the house. The confidence she possessed years before evolved into helplessness and she acquiesced to Walter's demands when he was home. When she met Jim, he rebuilt her self-assurance. He became her rescuer."

At first, Wolff said that she was intimidated by him. Apparently, his burly physique, deep booming voice, and abounding self-confidence overwhelmed her. If she had to come in to sign papers, she would call Wolff's paralegal, Jane, and ask if he was in the office. If he wasn't, Jane said JoAnn would quickly drive into Clayton before he returned and conduct whatever business needed to be done.

After the conversation he had with Dittmeier, Wolff called JoAnn to come in and talk over the possible plea bargain. The twins came with her. As they sat in his inner office, which resembled a bear's den, no windows and dim lighting, she sat erect in one of the chairs facing Wolff's cluttered desk.

"I don't want to plead to anything, Don. There's no evidence. Without that, they have no case."

"JoAnn, I know that. I believe you had nothing to do with Walter's murder, but do realize how antagonistic the press still feels about you?"

Bryan interjected, "Yeah, Mom. They crucified you. You know how that reporter for the Post-Dispatch always sat next to dad's parents and hugged them. Did one of them ever think what we were going through? They even came to school, badgering Mindy and me to make a statement about your arrest and Jim's."

"He's right, Mom," added Mindy wryly. "The press hates you. You wouldn't get a fair trial."

JoAnn looked at Wolff. "Yeah, now I'm known as the 'black widow.' I wonder how long it'll take to live that down?"

"It's not only the press, JoAnn. If Dittmeier takes this to trial, it would most likely be heard in St. Charles."

JoAnn said, "Well, we know I won't get a fair trial there. Everyone in St. Charles has made up his or her mind. But, damnit, Don, I don't want to give in to this."

"It's your decision, but is it worth the risk to forfeit five years as opposed to perhaps life, maybe even death?"

Mindy grabbed JoAnn's hand and Bryan put his arm around his mother's shoulders. Soon, all three of them were crying.

"Mom, we don't want to lose you forever. We've lost Dad. Jim's locked up for life. You're all we have," beseeched Bryan.

After drying her tears, she stared at the Duke Ellington pictures and other jazz memorabilia behind Wolff's desk. Then taking a deep breath, she asked, "How long would I actually be in?"

"On a five year felony sentence, you might serve eighteen months to two years. And listen, JoAnn, it's a lot better than the other alternative if we don't win."

Letting out a big sigh, she looked at her children, one on either side of her, smiled wanly at both, then told her attorney, "Okay, I'll agree. Let's go with it."

"It's a wise decision, JoAnn. Perhaps if you had gone to trial, you might have gotten off. But because of the slant the press and the television shows took on this, I sure wouldn't want to take the risk."

"I can't imagine what it'll be like in prison. God, what's happened to my life?" And again, JoAnn burst into tears.

■ ■ ■

After JoAnn agreed to the conditions of her reduced sentence, Dittmeier called Kay and Walter Notheis to inform them of the situation. Both of Walter's parents expressed extreme anger.

"Tom, we fought all these years to get justice for Wally. How can you do this to us? Don't you know what we've gone through?"

"Kay, I'm sorry. Believe me, if I could I would put forth a one hundred percent effort in trying this case. Although I have a lot of inadmissible evidence on JoAnn, I have very little that the court would allow. I know that a judge would throw the case out for lack of evidence."

"I don't care. You've got to try her."

"I wish I could, Kay, but again, there's simply not enough evidence to get a conviction. This way there won't be double jeopardy."

"What's that?"

"If I went to court and she's found not guilty, which is what would happen, she could never again be tried for Walter's murder. Even if she publicly admitted to it afterwards."

Only Kay's exasperated breathing could be heard over the phone.

Dittmeier continued. "This way, if some new evidence is revealed in the future, JoAnn could still be tried for Walter's murder."

Eventually, Dittmeier convinced Walter Scott's parents of his decision, yet for several years afterward they still clung to their bitterness.

▪ ▪ ▪

On February 1, 1993, JoAnn Marie Notheis Williams entered the courtroom holding Don Wolff's hand. In a low voice she told Judge Webber that she was aware that she would be sentenced to five years in prison and a five thousand dollar fine if she agreed to the charges of hindering the prosecution, contingent to the State dropping the first-degree murder charge in her former husband's death.

While the proceedings were going on, Kay and Walter Notheis looked emotionally drained as they sat a few rows behind their former daughter-in-law. Kay kept wiping away her tears. Occasionally, Walter would take out his handkerchief and blow his nose.

JoAnn left the courtroom with her children and a group of friends. She would remain free on a five hundred thousand dollar bond until her sentencing date on April 26, 1993, six years after the police pulled her first husband's body out of the cistern behind her second husband's house.

▪ ▪ ▪

The couple of months quickly passed. Snows melted. Leaves burst forth on trees. JoAnn once more entered the courtroom for her sentencing. Many of her friends and family members joined her in a unison of support. By now she had conditioned herself to spend time in jail. No longer did she have to hold her attorney's hand for a sense of security. Impassively looking at Judge Webber, she listened as he sentenced her. After explaining the conditions of her sentence, he then told her he would allow her two hours to be with her family and friends before she had to surrender herself to the St. Charles County Sheriff's Department.

Upon leaving the courthouse, Walter Notheis's second son, Scott, told the reporters, "My former step-mother got off real easy. She played all her cards just right. It's not fair."

But her attorney, Wolff, defended the sentence. "If she had gone to trial for capital murder, we probably couldn't find twelve people in St. Charles County who had not heard about this case, especially after Jim's trial. And despite the plea bargain, I don't think anyone can feel happy or good about going to prison."

▪ ▪ ▪

After court adjourned, Kay and Walter Notheis, along with other family members, went to a Denny's Restaurant in St. Charles for lunch. Because they had fifteen in their group, they asked the hostess if they could have the small, private banquet room which was partitioned off from the other diners. The hostess apologized, saying it was occupied.

While they waited for several tables to be cleared and pushed together to accommodate them, they talked about JoAnn. Everyone was upset that JoAnn's charge had been reduced. And to intensify this, they were angry that the judge had allowed her to leave for a few hours. Walter's first wife, Doris, joined her former in-laws. She didn't attend Jim's trial, but she wanted to be there at JoAnn's. She said, "Because JoAnn caused the divorce between Walter and me, I wanted to see her get some type of retribution."

Finally, the hostess seated them. As they were sitting around looking at the menus and talking, the banquet room's sliding partition door opened. JoAnn and Mindy stood in the doorway with Bryan and JoAnn's friends behind them.

Both groups stopped talking. Doris suddenly felt sick to her stomach. Wally, Jr., clenched the edge of the table. A female deputy, who the Court ordered to accompany JoAnn, noticed the potential confrontational situation and whispered to JoAnn. They quickly left. The irony of this accidental meeting shocked everyone.

▪ ▪ ▪

When Mike Krenski wrote "The Cheater" in the mid-60's, he was cognizant of human frailties. In all aspects of life most people "cheat" to some degree. It could start with school kids cheating on exams. Then it could escalate to cheating on income taxes. But in relationships it could mean having an affair. Walter cheated on both of his wives. Jim cheated on his. And JoAnn cheated on Walter. And sometimes the cheating goes far beyond an extramarital affair to murder. Just like in Krenski's song, that "cheater" ultimately turns out to be a fool-hearted clown. Eventually, something, someone will bring him or her down.

EPILOGUE

After serving eighteen months in a Missouri correctional institution for women, in October of 1994 JoAnn regained her freedom. Some people expressed outrage with her release. But Don Wolff said, "There's hard time, then soft time. When JoAnn entered prison, her self-esteem was nil. She went from a prestigious secretarial position at KMOX-TV to cleaning toilets in other people's homes to having people call her vile names. My client lost all sense of who she was, what her strengths were. Despite it being only eighteen months of actual time behind bars, she served hard time."

In jail, JoAnn met many women, from the young and vulnerable, who were behind bars for the first time, to the hardened convicts, who had forgotten what is was to be hopeful about life. But she adjusted. She had to in order to survive.

Because she's an intelligent woman, and many of the inmates were illiterate, she began teaching some of them to read. Slowly, she even allowed herself to become friends with a few women. She listened to their problems and offered advice.

In her deep, husky voice, she said, "When I went to prison, I didn't think I'd live through it. In fact, all of us, everyone, Walter's mother and father, his boys, my kids, all of us have been through hell. But I've learned that everything is for a reason. I've made some very unwise choices in the past. Now, I carefully consider my decisions regarding almost everything."

Wolff said that when JoAnn met with him after she got out of prison, she was like a different woman. No longer did she blanch at his assertive manner. No longer was she emotionally frail. "She earned back her self-esteem, her self-respect, which she hadn't had for many years."

Upon leaving prison, JoAnn moved into an apartment with her daughter, Mindy, who attended a university out of the St. Louis area. She found employment and also began attending psychological therapy sessions. A couple of weekends a month, she drives to St. Charles to visit her son. Occasionally, she visits her husband, Jim Williams, at the Potosi Correctional Center.

▪ ▪ ▪

After his conviction, Jim Williams spent seven weeks in the St. Charles County jail. He knew the guards. He was familiar with the rules. Then in January, 1993, when the judge concurred with the jurors' sentence, a high security van transported him ninety miles southwest to the hilly rural area of Mineral Point. Two hours after leaving St. Charles, the van crested a hill, and looming in front of Jim was the Potosi Correctional Institution, a maximum security prison in Missouri where most of the state's murderers are incarcerated, either serving life sentences or awaiting their deaths.

The perimeter is surrounded by several twenty foot fences with rows upon rows of razor-sharp circular barbed wire attached horizontally and vertically to the top, bottom and middle of the chained links. Guards stand armed in the tall tower, scouring the two-laned road and rolling fields around the prison. Prison officers frequently walk the parking area checking cars. And numerous electronic cameras surveil everyone, from the parking lot to the visiting rooms to even the visitors' bathrooms.

For the first four days, the officials put Jim in a cell by himself, similar to lockdown. It's a normal procedure for new prisoners so they can gradually adjust to the facility, and also so the prison officials can observe the psychological reactions of an inmate.

After being placed within the general population, Jim was assigned to work in the cafeteria as a cook. Three days passed before other inmates challenged the rookie. He finished cooking breakfast and went out to the track to walk six laps. Several hundred feet in front of him, three inmates sat by a manhole cover. They kept staring at Jim as he approached. When he passed, they got up and followed. He knew this would be his first confrontation.

Soon, the three surrounded him. "Mr. Williams," said one of the men menacingly, "We need to talk to you."

Jim's eyes narrowed. "Okay, get with the program."

"Under the circumstances in which you came in here, and the type of trial you had, we think that you need protection."

"Uh, huh, and suppose I refuse?"

The spokesperson for the trio responded, "Well, you could get hurt."

With a sinister look in his eyes, Jim replied, "I'll tell you something right now. You decide among the three of you which one of you wants to die, because one of you is going to die this morning. So, whichever one wants to go first, just jump right in here."

After staring at Jim's six foot six inch frame, his large girth, and ominous eyes, one of them turned and hurried back to the building, while the other two slowly retreated, their eyes glued on Jim. From that day on, no one else tested him.

When he's not working in the supply shop of the prison's factory, he goes to the library to read and often to write letters. A lot of letters. Frequently, he visits with several inmates who have developed paralegal skills and who assist him in his appeals. He had managed a softball team in prison, but gave that up once he developed arthritis in his knees. At night he watches television, and on weekends he goes to the recording studio at the prison and records country and country gospel music.

While being in Potosi, he says he's not as friendly as he used to be. He seldom visits other inmates and doesn't want them in his "house." Ironically, one of the other prisoners he became friends with is Ed Post, a former New Orleans realtor who visited St. Louis for a convention. He drowned his wife in the hotel's tub and was convicted of her murder.

Jim still reminisces about the past. When talking about his grandfather or JoAnn, his eyes well up with sadness. "My grandfather and my wife were my best friends. I loved my first wife, Sharon, yet we weren't really good friends. But JoAnn and I love each other. Our lives together really meant something."

Recalling his trial, he feels something happened to change its course. His attorney, Mike Turken, assured him that they had it won. But one day after a two hour lunch recess, Jim said, "Turken came back into the courtroom looking like a whipped dog with his tail between his legs. From that point on, things went downhill."

Although Dittmeier's position in the case was to convict Jim of murdering Sharon and Walter, Jim stated, "He's a fantastic lawyer. Highly intelligent. And he has a great memory. During the trial he only had a legal pad and pen. He even knew each juror by name. He had everything locked in his head and never had to look at any notes."

Jim continues to maintain his innocence. Although he admits to shaking Sharon during arguments, he says he had never hit her. He still insists he was home at the time of her accident.

Regarding Walter's death, he contends he did not kill him.

He said that because he was raised on a farm and slaughtered many farm animals that if he had murdered Walter, he's smart enough to know that all he had to do was pour fifty pounds of lye over the body to get rid of the evidence.

He has had three appeals turned down, and is on his fourth.

▪ ▪ ▪

No parent wants to outlive his or her own child, whether the child be four, or in Walter's case, forty years old. Not only did Kay and Walter have to endure their son's death, but also the vile manner in which he was murdered. Besides having to confront deep heartache over their son's demise, they also had to persevere in getting justice served.

Kay said during the years of trying to get her son's murder case to trial, she reached a point when she plummeted into deep despair and hopelessness. With a heavy heart she prayed to God to take over, that she didn't know what else she and her husband could to do. A few days later the state's attorney general's office appointed Tom Dittmeier as the special prosecutor.

During Jim's trial, Kay said that Jim never looked at them once. Afterwards, she stated, "It's a weird feeling you get. There's no sense of relief, except that it's over. I was disappointed I didn't feel anything more." When their former daughter-in-law's charge of murder was reduced to hindering the prosecution, they were outraged.

Walter's parents were also angry that one year after Jim was sentenced, he was back in court trying to get a new trial. It took Kay and Walter five years from the time the police discovered their son's body in Jim's cistern to get the case to trial. And if they had not been so persistent, they doubted the case would have ever been tried.

Although Kay and Walter's bitterness is still understandably evident, Kay said she no longer believes in the death penalty. "What does taking one life for another prove? Nothing. Everyone will get their justice in the end."

Kay and Walter are currently in their seventies, both spry and active in various organizations and their church. They also continue to attend monthly meetings of the Parents of Murdered Children's group and are frequently seen at St. Louis murder trials, sitting with the family of the murdered victims and lending them emotional support.

Several times a month they visit the mausoleum where Walter is interred. They alternate from silent prayers to holding one-sided conversations with their son, telling him about what's going on in their lives and hearts. As they are ready to leave, they tell him they love him. Then they kiss their fingertips and pat the star on the front of Walter's vault.

▪ ▪ ▪

Because no one has openly admitted murdering Sharon Elaine Williams and Walter Simon Notheis, Jr., very few people actually know what happened on the nights of October 19, 1983, and December 27, 1983. Many questions go unanswered. If Jim did fatally injure his wife, then who quickly drove him back to his home within half an hour after Sharon's car was discovered down an embankment? Who helped Jim get Walter in a place where Walter would not suspect any foul play? Who actually pulled the trigger, shooting Walter in the back? And who drove Jim back to St. Charles after Walter's car was left at the airport? Obviously, Jim did not act alone. Perhaps one day the truth will be uncovered.

ORDER FORM

Telephone and Fax orders: 1-800-879-4214 (24 hour service)

Postal orders: Tula Publishing, Inc., Attn: Mark Dickherber,
P.O. Box 1544, St. Peters, MO 63376

Please send THE CHEATERS: THE WALTER SCOTT MURDER

Name: ______________________________

Address: ______________________________

City: ______________ State: _____ Zip: __________

Telephone: Area Code (   ) ______________________

Price of book @ $10.95 #Copies______ __________
(20% discount for 5 or more)

Missouri state sales tax @ $.63 per book __________
(For books shipped to Missouri addresses only)

Handling and shipping @ $3.00 per book __________

TOTAL to be remitted __________

Payment:
______Check ______Money Order Credit card: ______VISA

______MasterCard ______American Express ______Discover

Card Number: ______________________________

Name on card: ______________________________

Expiration date: ______________

Signature: ______________________________

Please allow 2-4 weeks for delivery.

Photo by Michael Sewell

Scottie Priesmeyer has written for a newspaper, won awards for her poetry and short stories, wrote a non-fiction historical book and a novel. She has a master's degree in English and teaches literature and writing classes part-time at a St. Louis college.